D0984301

CUSHING

MILITARY PROFILES
SERIES EDITOR
Dennis E. Showalter, Ph.D.
Colorado College

*Instructive summaries for general and expert
readers alike, volumes in the Military Profiles
series are essential treatments of significant and
popular military figures drawn from world history,
ancient times through the present.*

CUSHING

Civil War SEAL

Robert J. Schneller

BRASSEY'S, INC.
Washington, D.C.

Library of Congress Cataloging-in-Publication Data

Schneller, Robert John, 1957–
    Cushing : Civil War SEAL / Robert J. Schneller, Jr.—1st ed.
      p.   cm. — (Military profiles)
    Includes bibliographical references (p.) and index.
    ISBN 1-57488-506-5 (acid-free paper)—ISBN 1-57488-696-7 (pbk. : acid-free paper)
    1. Cushing, William Barker, 1842–1874. 2. Ship captains—United States—Biography. 3. United States. Navy—Officers—Biography. 4. United States—History—Civil War, 1861–1865—Naval operations. 5. United States—History—Civil War, 1861–1865—Commando operations. I. Title. II. Series.

   E467.1.C98S36   2003
   973.7'58'092—dc21   2003012137

Hardcover ISBN 1-57488-506-5
Softcover ISBN 1-57488-696-7
(alk. paper)

Brassey's, Inc.
22841 Quicksilver Drive
Dulles, Virginia 20166

FIRST EDITION

10 9 8 7 6 5 4 3 2 1

To Hayley and Walker

Contents

Maps

Preface

It was David versus Goliath, 1864 style, as the little Yankee picket boat moved in against the big rebel ironclad to kill or be killed. Before embarking on this mission, Will Cushing had bragged that he would "come out victorious or 'toes up.'"[1] The outcome would be decided in the next few minutes of that dark and stormy night. From his exposed position in the picket boat's bow, Cushing stared straight down the barrel of a 6.4-inch rifled cannon while struggling with a complicated device to detonate a torpedo, as mines were called in those days, under the ironclad's hull. Above the shouts of the Confederate soldiers ashore and the din of their firing, he could hear the gun captain on the ironclad issuing orders to the crew. In only seconds they would fire. Even as bullets tore through his clothing, Cushing coolly counted to five while the torpedo moved into position, then pulled the lanyard. The roar of simultaneous explosions filled his ears. The round from the Confederate cannon flew over his head. The torpedo threw up an immense column of water, which seemed to flatten out the picket boat like a pasteboard box. But it also blew a hole in the bottom of the ironclad big enough to drive a wagon through and sent her to the bottom. Cushing dove into the cold river and made good his escape. It seemed a miracle he wasn't killed, but impossible missions and narrow escapes were his forte.

William Barker Cushing (1842–74) was one of the most daring men in American naval history. Like men of today's Navy Sea-Air-Land (SEAL) teams, he excelled at raids behind enemy lines, missions that today are called special operations, and he was better at it than any of his contemporaries, Union or Confederate. During the Civil War, he always seemed to be planning, executing, or recovering from raids to cut out enemy vessels, burn facilities ashore, or gather intelligence. During these missions he fought all manner of rebel forces, from regular cavalry, artillery, and infantry to guerrillas. By the end of the war, he had amassed four commendations from the Navy Department and the thanks of Congress and President Lincoln. All this by a man who was only twenty-two years old when Lee surrendered at Appomattox.

Cushing's ego was as big as the great outdoors. He was patriotic, aggressive, tough, and recklessly bold. He disdained people who lacked these qualities. His bravery was matched only by his own bad temper. Once an officer refused to let him lead a mission to capture a particular enemy steamer, which subsequently escaped. "Instead of the blue and gold of a dashing service," Cushing said of the officer in his memoirs, "he should have worn petticoats."[2] After the war a newspaper editor described Cushing as an "idiotic young snob" and "egotistical ass."[3] After reading the account Cushing strode into the editor's office and lashed him with a rawhide whip. One of the men whom Cushing led on the raid to sink the *Albemarle* described him best. "His eye was peculiarly piercing and very direct," he said after the war in a speech to a veteran's organization. "He seemed to be looking through the man he was talking with, and his glance to a stranger was a kind of challenge."[4]

This is a military biography of Cushing, not a full biography. It dwells neither on his personal relationships nor on his life during peacetime. The focus remains on the daring operations he conducted during the Civil War, as well as on those aspects of his personality that drove him to take such risks.

Many people helped me with this book. I thank Rick Russell, who signed me again for the Military Profiles series. As always, my agent, Fritz Heinzen, has my gratitude for his friendship and guidance. I'm indebted to Chris Fonvielle and, as usual, Bob Browning and Mark Hayes for suffering through a draft of the entire book and offering valuable suggestions for its improvement.

I thank the staffs of the Chautauqua County Historical Society in Westfield, New York; the Historical Museum of the State Historical Society of Wisconsin in Madison, Wisconsin; the D. R. Barker Library in Fredonia, New York; the National Archives; and the Library of Congress for providing documents and photographs. The staffs of the Naval Historical Foundation and the Naval Historical Center's Photographic Section also have my gratitude for their assistance with illustrations. I remain grateful to Barbara Auman, Davis Elliott, Glenn Helm, Jean Hort, Young Park, and Tonya Simpson of the Navy Department Library for granting my constant requests for books and documents and answering countless reference questions. Although these people helped make this book better, responsibility for its flaws remains with me.

Last but not least, I want to thank my wife, Rebecca, and sons, Zachary and Noah, for their patience and support during the time I spent with Cushing and not with them.

Chronology

1842	Cushing is born in Wisconsin on November 4.
1857	Cushing is appointed acting midshipman on September 25.
1861	His resignation from the Navy is accepted on March 23. On April 1, he is appointed to serve as master's mate on the *Minnesota*. On September 13, he resigns again. On October 19, Cushing is warranted a midshipman, dating from June 1. On October 25, he is ordered to North Atlantic Blockading Squadron (NABS). On November 6, he assists in destroying the *Ada* in the Rappahannock River.
1862	On March 23, Cushing is detached from the *Cambridge*. He is ordered to the *Minnesota* on May 14 and promoted to lieutenant on July 16. On October 3, Cushing participates in an engagement in the Blackwater River, where he is placed in command of the *Ellis*.
1863	From April 11 to May 4, Cushing is senior officer in charge of gunboats cooperating with the Army in defense of Suffolk, Virginia. On September 5, he is detached from the *Shokokon* to command the *Monticello*.
1864	On October 27, Cushing sinks the CSS *Albemarle* and is promoted to lieutenant commander as a result. He takes command of the USS *Malvern*, Porter's flagship, on December 2 and on December

	20 receives the thanks of Congress for destroying the *Albemarle*. On December 24–25, the first Fort Fisher expedition fails, and on December 27 Cushing resumes command of the *Monticello*.
1865	Union forces capture Fort Fisher on December 20. On February 24, Cushing is detached from the *Monticello*, and on May 17, he is ordered to the navy yard in New York. On June 24, he is ordered to the *Lancaster*, Pacific Squadron.
1867	On March 11, Cushing is detached from the *Lancaster* and awaiting orders. On October 7, he is ordered to command the *Maumee*.
1869	Cushing is detached from the *Maumee* on November 12.
1870	On February 22, Cushing marries Katherine Louise Forbes. On March 30, he is ordered to ordnance duty at the Boston Navy Yard.
1872	Cushing is promoted to commander on January 31. On February 9, he is detached from the Boston Navy Yard and awaits orders.
1873	On July 11, he is ordered to command the *Wyoming*.
1874	Detached and awaiting orders on April 24, Cushing is ordered as assistant to executive officer, Washington Navy Yard, on April 27. On August 25, he is ordered as senior aid to the commandant of the Washington Navy Yard. Cushing dies on December 17 at the Government Hospital for the Insane in Washington, D.C.

CUSHING

VIRGINIA

Currituck Inlet

Dismal Swamp

Elizabeth City

NORTH

Roanoke River

Chowan River

Albemarle Sound

Roanoke Island

Old Inlet
Oregon Inlet
Ft. Oregon

Plymouth

New Inlet

★ RALEIGH

Tar River

CAROLINA

Pamlico River

Pamlico Sound

Goldsboro

Kinston

Neuse River

Cape Hatteras

Fts. Hatteras and Clark

West Inlet

Hatteras Inlet

Outer Shoals

New Bern

Neuse River

Ocracoke Inlet

Wilmington & Weldon RR

New River

Onslow C.H. (Jacksonville)

Morehead City

Whitehall

Virginia Cr.

Bogue Inlet

Cape Lookout

South River

Lookout Breakers

Cape Fear River

New Topsail Inlet

Wilmington

Coast and Sounds
of
North Carolina

Ft. Fisher

Ft. Caswell

Cape Fear

Frying Pan Shoals

Statute Miles

0   10   20   30   40   50

Karamales 2003

Swampy area

Chapter 1

Restless Child

T HE NOVEMBER WIND rustling through the tall prairie grass in southeastern Wisconsin carried the sting of approaching winter. Inside the cozy log cabin, Mary Barker Cushing couldn't have cared less about the weather as she struggled to give birth to her sixth son. When her labor ended, the infant was placed in her arms. She looked him over carefully. He seemed healthy. A wave of joy and relief washed over her. She and her husband named the baby William Barker Cushing.

Will Cushing came from a family of restless adventurers. Zattu Cushing, Will's grandfather, was born in Plymouth, Massachusetts, in 1770. When Zattu was seven years old, he heard that General Burgoyne had surrendered at Saratoga. He set out from school in Plymouth in the middle of the night, "walking, running, and leaping for joy" across ten miles of fields and woodlands to his family's farm to bring home news of the victory.[1]

When his father lost the farm because of the inflation that followed in the wake of the Revolutionary War, Zattu left Massachusetts and went west to the backwoods of New York, where in

1805 he settled in the town of Fredonia, which stood some three or four miles inland from the shores of Lake Erie. By then he had been married ten years and had fathered five children. A neighbor said that his most prominent characteristics were "restless energy and an indomitable will."[2] Zattu had been a farmer and a shipbuilder, and he soon received the appointment of associate justice of Niagara County Court. He attended all the sessions of the court in Buffalo, rose to become the court's leading member, and presided at the most important trials. When Chautauqua County separated from Niagara County in 1811, he became the new county's chief judge.

In 1825 Zattu retired from the bench to exploit opportunities arising from the Erie Canal, which opened to commerce that October, linking the frontier to New York City. Over the next year he and other citizens of Fredonia built a canal boat in a pasture north of his house. The boat carried the first wheat sent from Chautauqua County to New York City. Zattu spent his remaining years in business. He died peacefully in his bed on January 13, 1839.

Zattu's son Milton Buckingham Cushing, born in 1800 and raised in Fredonia, earned a degree in medicine and set up a practice in Zanesville, Ohio. There he married his first wife, Abigail Tupper, who bore him two sons and two daughters. Although handsome and charming, Milton was thin, nervous and not terribly robust. When the rigors of being a physician proved too much for him, he left medicine and went into business, eventually settling in Columbus, Ohio. One tragedy after another befell the family. Abigail died in 1833, leaving four children, who also died young. Their two daughters lived only long enough to marry. Both sons perished in their middle twenties.

Although not physically strong, Milton was fortunate to have inherited his father's steely character. His intelligence and energy more than made up for his physical frailty. He was a clear-sighted businessman, a devoted friend, and a charitable and politically active citizen. An opponent of slavery, he gave liberally of his time and money to the cause of freedom. All in all, he remained a great catch and married again in 1836.

Mary Barker Smith had a similarly steely character, no doubt stemming in part from the blood she shared with the families of John Adams, John Hancock, and James Madison. Unlike Milton, she was physically strong and loved living close to nature. She hailed from Boston and was visiting relatives in Columbus when she met Milton. She was twenty-nine when they married.

While raising the children of Milton's first marriage, Mary bore him six more sons and another daughter. Two of Mary's sons didn't survive childhood. Her fifth and sixth sons would achieve renown: Alonzo Hersford, born in January 1841, and Will, born twenty-one months later on November 4, 1842.

Milton had also inherited Zattu's restlessness and kept the family moving as it grew. In 1837, the Cushings moved from Ohio to Wisconsin, first to Milwaukee, then, in 1839, to a log cabin in a village in the center of a valley twelve miles north of Prairieville (now Waukesha). It was frontier living, with Potawatomi Indians still fishing and hunting nearby.

Here Milton regained a measure of health and his medical degree made him one of the most educated men in the village. He was appointed justice of the peace, and when the village was incorporated under the name of Nemahbin (now Delafield), he became chairman of its first board of supervisors. Nemahbin had no store or post office when Will was born. Twice a month, weather permitting, the Cushings took an oxcart to Prairieville to replenish their stock of flour, sugar, and whatnot.

It wasn't long before the rigors of frontier living proved too much for Milton's frail constitution. In 1844 he moved the family to the waterfront of Chicago, where he returned to medicine. He soon built a thriving practice. In the fall of 1846 Dr. Cushing's health deteriorated, and he decided to travel south for a gentler clime. He spent the winter in Vicksburg, Mississippi, at a cousin's home. He got somewhat better and started back north in the spring. But he had made it only as far as Gallipolis, Ohio, when he came down with pneumonia and died in a hotel bed on

April 22, 1847. Mary Cushing went down to pick up his body and had him buried in Fredonia.

Early that summer, Mary Cushing moved her family back to Fredonia from Chicago. With only a small amount of money available from her inheritance and her in-laws, Mary started a school in her home. The older boys got jobs after school to help out.

With everyone else working to support the family, Will and Allie, as his brother was affectionately called, became inseparable. Nevertheless, they differed in their views of the world. Whereas Allie approached an undertaking by worrying about the problems that might arise along the way, Will never doubted that he could turn his wishes into reality.

Later that summer, Mary gave Will money for rail fare to the neighboring town of Silver Creek to visit his aunt. Will liked this aunt so much that he spent all the money on a gift for her. He boarded the train with empty pockets, perhaps even without trepidation, and sat down next to a well-dressed, kind-looking gentleman. Will struck up a conversation, charming the old fellow with an account of the duck eggs he and Allie had found the day before. When the conductor came around to collect the fare, Will reached into his pocket as if to get money, but the gentleman insisted on paying the boy's way. Mrs. Cushing didn't learn of the feat until months later, when her sister mentioned the beautiful gift Will had given her.

Will showed signs of being a born leader early on. He often imposed his will on the other boys in town. Once he formed an organization dubbed the "Muss Company," which existed briefly until its noontime musters outside the school interfered with the schoolmaster's authority. "Will was the ringleader in all the berrying, nutting and fishing frolics," his sister Mary Isabel later recalled, "and our adventures would fill a volume. He always killed every snake, even pulling them out of their holes." Isabel also recalled when a cousin sent Will to take an ill horse to a pasture in the neighboring town of Awkright. "He found an old wagon," she noted, "and taking a lot of us children, went to

Awkright for a berrying. At every hill, great or small, we were all under orders to alight and help the horse to get the wagon up the hill."[3]

Will grew bolder as he grew older. He rode horses faster, climbed trees higher, and swam farther than the other boys in Fredonia. He did it for the thrill and to maintain his position at the top of the pecking order. The pastor's daughter remembered Will as a "venturesome" lad and "a daring and willful leader of his young companions. He was quick tempered and always ready to settle disputes with a fight, upon the principle that the best men won the battle."[4]

In 1855 Will's uncle, Francis Smith Edwards, lined up a job for him as a page in the House of Representatives. Congressman Edwards represented New York State's thirty-fourth district. Since the job was slated to begin the next summer, Uncle Francis said, Will needed to do as much school work as possible in the interim.

Fredonia had several grade schools, a public high school, and an academy on Elm Street. After finishing school most kids went to work, except for the rare boy who headed east to college at Colgate, Harvard, or Yale. Will studied enough mathematics, Latin, and American history to graduate from Fredonia Academy in June 1856. That fall he left for Washington.

At first Will lived with his aunt and uncle in their suite of rooms near the unfinished Capitol. When not at work, Will spent as much time as possible with his beloved cousin Mary. After Uncle Francis lost the election that November, Will moved to Washington House, where the other pages resided.

Will found his job less congenial than his living arrangements. It was not that the work was hard. It demanded nothing more than being present on the House floor during debates and being available to carry messages for congressmen. The difficulty for Will lay in the fact that with so many pages available, he had to spend a large portion of each day sitting still and keeping quiet, neither of which befitted his restless nature. Listening to the debates didn't help. "I heard enough nonsense in my time in the House to last for fifty years," he later recalled.[5] Still, he did his job well enough and impressed both his peers and employers with his total self-confidence and gift of gab.

The great redeeming characteristic of working in Washington was the chance to meet, or at least to observe, the men who ran the country. Despite his disdain for debates in the House, he sometimes watched debates in the Senate, just to see whom he could see. On March 4, 1857, Will had a grandstand seat for the inauguration of President James Buchanan, one of the day's dimmest leading lights.

In terms of Will's immediate future, the most important person he met in Washington was Commodore (later Rear Admiral) Joseph Smith, one of the United States Navy's top officers. As head of the Bureau of Yards and Docks since 1846, Smith oversaw warship construction during the period when steam propulsion was revolutionizing the Navy. Since Smith was Mary Cushing's cousin, he did what he could to help the hard-working widow's family. Between the efforts of the commodore cousin with the "frighteningly serious demeanor"[6] and the outgoing congressman Uncle Francis, in the spring of 1857 Will received an appointment to the United States Naval Academy.

Will returned home to Fredonia briefly before going off to Annapolis. Allie was home, too. Uncle Francis had arranged an appointment for Allie to the United States Military Academy in West Point, New York. Will and Allie spent their time together talking about military and naval history and teasing each other about their respective chosen service.

When the time came for Will to leave home for the Naval Academy, he donned his best clothes and went around Fredonia calling on friends, neighbors, and relatives to say goodbye. Mary Cushing, Isabel, and cousin George White drove him to Dunkirk, where he caught the train to Buffalo, and from there to New York City. Will spent a couple of days in the big city, then boarded a train for Annapolis by way of Philadelphia and Baltimore.

Chapter 2

Mischievous Midshipman

O<small>N SEPTEMBER</small> 25, 1857, Will Cushing and seventy-three other boys were sworn as acting midshipmen into the class of 1861. Those who went on to graduate would receive midshipman warrants, the ticket to the bottom rung of the officer corps ladder. Since only academy graduates could receive warrants and only warranted midshipmen could climb to higher rank, the academy was the Navy's sole source of line officers and the fount of the officer corps in those days.

Back home in Fredonia, Will had been the undisputed leader of his peers. In Annapolis, he found himself among dozens of other lads who had been leaders in their own hometowns and were destined to become the leaders of the Navy. The competition was fierce.

The upper classes present when Will was sworn in included the classes of 1858, 1859, and 1860. Thirteen of the sixty graduates of these classes would reach flag rank. Among the most famous were George Dewey, class of 1858, whose lopsided victory in the battle of Manila Bay during the Spanish-American War would earn him the rank of admiral of the Navy; Alfred Thayer Mahan, class of 1859, a brilliant, but unpopular, man who hated going to sea, but who would become the nineteenth century's greatest naval historian; and Winfield Scott Schley, class of 1860, who would have operational command of a squadron of warships during the other great American naval victory of the Spanish-American War, the Battle of Santiago.

The leading light among Cushing's classmates was William T. Sampson, one of five '61 alumni who went on to make flag rank. Sampson would graduate first in his class, become architect of the victory at Santiago, and engage Schley in a bitter struggle over the credit for it. Cushing remained the youngest midshipman at the academy until his third year.

Cushing himself was an upperclassman when the classes of 1862, 1863, and 1864 were sworn in. The 137 graduates of these three classes included nearly three dozen future flag officers. The top graduate of 1862, Samuel William Preston, numbered among Will's best friends at the academy. Benjamin Horton Porter, class of 1863, was also one of Cushing's best friends. The class of 1864 included Robley D. Evans, a man whose pugnacity matched Cushing's and would earn him the appellation "Fighting Bob."[1] They were destined for triumph and tragedy in the coming war.

While these future leaders were still midshipmen, however, the academy's military, academic, and disciplinary standards constituted the yardsticks by which they were measured. Military discipline shaped diverse groups of boys into junior officers who thought and acted alike. Regulations subordinated midshipmen to their instructors, required them to wear uniforms at all times while attached to the academy, imposed mandatory formations, established a hierarchy of midshipman officers, and organized the midshipmen man-o'-war fashion into gun crews, which became companies for infantry drill. The regulations forbade dueling and card playing; possession of firearms, alcoholic beverages, and tobacco; marriage; and contracting unauthorized debts. Other proscribed activities included lounging on beds during the day, sitting on the steps of halls or buildings, and hanging pictures or maps on dormitory room walls without the commandant's permission. Beds had to be made and rooms cleaned before breakfast. No one, including officers and professors, was allowed to go outside the academy's walls without the superintendent's permission.

The metamorphosis from civilian to midshipman took place abruptly during the first, or "plebe," year. The initial shock of isolation from familiar surroundings, coupled with the total immersion in naval life, customs, and traditions, with its identical routines, quarters, food, uniforms, and discipline, stripped midshipmen of diverse regional thought and behavior patterns and clad them in uniform, more cosmopolitan, and distinctly naval cultural raiment. "When you enter the Academy you cease to be a Vermonter or a Georgian or a Californian," wrote George Dewey. "You are in the Navy; your future, with its sea-service and its frequent changes of assignment, makes you first a man of the country's service and only secondly a man of the world."[2]

The academy imbued officers with an ethic of renouncing worldly gain in favor of service, much like the ministry. This ethic made naval officers very sensitive to affronts to their honor and, more importantly, to the nation's honor. Naval officers' prestige stemmed from their identification with something bigger than themselves, their Navy and their country. "None but a naval officer could fully understand the devotion of another officer to their common profession," wrote Thomas O. Selfridge Jr., class of 1854, in his memoirs. "The close unity of thought and action that binds our profession into a great fraternity has no parallel among civilians."[3] Cushing reflected this feeling in letters to loved ones by referring to classmates as "bro. middies."[4]

Before a man could serve his country in the Navy, however, he had to survive the academy's weeding-out process. Attrition was high. Only 45 percent of the midshipmen admitted into the academy between 1854 and 1860 succeeded in graduating.

Much of the weeding out took place in the classroom. By 1859 the faculty numbered fourteen civilians and nearly as many officers. Midshipmen took courses in nine departments: seamanship, gunnery, and naval tactics; mathematics; astronomy, navigation, and surveying; natural and experimental philosophy (science); field artillery and infantry tactics; ethics and English studies; drawing; French; and Spanish. Professors graded midshipmen's work on a four-point scale, with a 4.0 being the best grade and a 2.5 needed to pass. Although the curriculum bore a vague resemblance to that found in civilian colleges, it placed greater emphasis on naval subjects like seamanship, navigation, and gunnery than on general subjects like English and foreign languages. Textbooks glorified obedience to the country and promoted respect for order, race, and rank. Outside the classroom, midshipmen learned fencing, marching, ship rigging, and other naval and military skills.

Cushing didn't distinguish himself academically. It wasn't that he found the courses terribly difficult; he simply didn't devote much time to studying. Yet, he still managed to earn reasonably good grades. In his junior year, he stood third in gunnery, eighth in ethics, thirteenth in astronomy, and ninth in general order of merit out of a class of thirty-seven.

Some intellectual pursuits did capture his interest. The Lawrence Literary Society, a debating club, met once a week in the lyceum. Arguing with his peers suited his combative nature, and Cushing became a leading member. His later fluency in addressing public gatherings resulted in part from this experience.

Like many people of that era, Cushing liked to exchange letters with loved ones. Perhaps his favorite correspondent during his stay at the Naval Academy was his cousin Mary Edwards. Neatness of penmanship, clarity of expression, and a touch of romanticism to counterbalance the machismo of his relationships with men marked Will's letters to his beloved cousin Mary, many of which he signed, "Your affectionate cousin, Will." "You contribute to my happiness by writing," he once wrote her. "I get hardly any of the gossip from the village," he added, "do give me a little."[5] One of Cousin Mary's letters arrived during a particularly difficult time. "You can have no idea of the pleasure with which I then read your welcome letter," Will replied. "It was, for the time, both sleep and food, and I returned to duty very much refreshed."[6]

For the most part, however, academy life bored Cushing. Men of action like Will found relief from classroom droning in mischief. In quarters, they sometimes set pails of water atop doors to douse duty officers. Occasionally, they would load the morning gun with bricks. In chapel they were given to passing the bottle while praising the Lord.

Cushing became one of the academy's leading pranksters. One of his favorite tricks, as he put it in a letter to Cousin Mary, was "the art of extinguishing all the gas light in the building during study hours by vigorously blowing into a burner."[7] No doubt pandemonium would ensue.

One of Will's more famous pranks was dubbed "the tea party." Cooks customarily brewed bucketfuls of tea for the evening meal and set them on the kitchen windowsills to cool. Every now and then, Will would go fishing for the tea from a window above, dropping a line down, hooking a bucket, and hauling in the catch. He and several companions would drink their fill and pour out the rest. Then, they would refill the buckets with water, and Will would lower them back down to the kitchen windowsill. The chief cook never did catch on.

Occasionally, Cushing took the prank a step further, filling old whiskey bottles with the brown liquid. In the morning room inspectors would find the bottles and haul him before the superintendent. Cushing would act innocent, which he was, for there was no rule forbidding tea in a midshipman's room.

Another of Will's most famous pranks unfolded at the expense of a drill instructor who stuttered. One fine day in March 1859, the drill instructor was drilling Will and his classmates in field artillery marching along the bank of the Severn. The bank turned, and the drill instructor attempted to turn the midshipmen, but he began stuttering and couldn't get the order out. A smirk flashed onto Cushing's face. He continued marching forward, leading his comrades, guns and all, into the river.

Restless midshipmen like Cushing also relieved boredom by "Frenching it," the term for leaving the yard without permission. The objective of a Frenching expedition was usually one of the taverns or pool halls just outside the academy's number-one gate in the Hell Point section of town. Here the opportunities for getting into trouble far exceeded those available inside the yard. According to one old timer, the "grog shops" there "were dives of vice and rendezvous of the ruffians, murderers and bullies of a rare type."[8] Occasionally, midshipmen mixed it up with youth gangs from town, often over girls.

Cushing became an expert at Frenching it. He learned the habits of the watchstanders and could outrun those whom he couldn't evade, with one notable exception. The police force for keeping midshipmen in the yard and out of trouble included a large black Newfoundland dog let loose to roam the grounds inside the walls by night. Try as he might, Cushing failed to befriend the dog, so he did his best to avoid the animal. He mostly proved successful, although on one occasion the dog managed to tear out the seat of his pants. "Fortunately," he wrote Cousin Mary, "they were by no means my best pair of trousers."[9]

Cushing certainly didn't get away with everything. In fact, he got caught breaking the regulations rather frequently. Punishments for infractions ranged from restriction and demerits to dismissal. A midshipman who accumulated two hundred demerits in the course of a year was automatically dismissed. During his first year Cushing received ninety-nine. The next year he teetered on the brink, accumulating 188 demerits for minor infractions and ranking last in his class in conduct. In his third and fourth years Cushing stepped back from the brink, tallying, respectively, 155 and 147 demerits. His infractions included things like oversleeping, absence from roll call, and absence from chapel. None of his offenses were serious.

Cushing's keen mind, high spirits, and devil-may-care attitude about breaking the rules and taking his punishment made him popular among his peers. So did his generosity. In February 1861, his mother sent him a box full of Fredonia produce, including apples, maple sugar, and preserves—a sort of nineteenth century care package. He gave most of it away the day he received it.

The Naval Academy's rigorous schedule included its share of breaks, during which Will visited friends and relatives. During his second year, Cushing once visited an aunt who lived in Chelsea, Massachusetts. A boy from the neighborhood poked fun at his short uniform jacket. The insult provoked Cushing to fight. The battle turned bloody as it "raged over the sidewalks and dusty streets," as the aunt put it in a letter to Mrs. Cushing, but Will won.[10] Nobody else made fun of him during the visit.

Despite his abhorrence for academics and distaste for discipline, the academy succeeded in channeling Cushing's restlessness, optimism, and lust for adventure into the ideals of the naval officer. It wasn't the classroom that imbued Cushing with the Navy's ideals, but the quarterdeck. Each summer the first and third classes set sail on a bona fide warship for a practice cruise, designed to teach them to sail and fight a warship. After finishing final examinations in June, the midshipmen boarded the practice ship, were assigned watch stations, lockers, and mess seats, and divided into gun crews. They spent their days on deck standing watches, aloft working the sails, below deck studying seamanship and navigation, and mustering for man-overboard, fire, collision, and abandon-ship drills. The seniors took turns as deck officers and navigators. Summer practice cruises embodied all the dangers inherent to a life at sea. All in all, they made for excellent training. Midshipmen on practice cruises were required to do all of the work on the ship, even the most menial.

While academic work bored Cushing, service afloat utterly enthralled and inspired him. Whether because of the salt air, the grandeur of the sea, or the leadership role for which he was preparing, Cushing thrived at sea and reveled in its danger. In the spring of 1860, he penned his cousin a letter that reflects both his longing for the sea and the degree to which he had imbibed the spirit of the Navy as bottled at Annapolis:

You say that you almost envy me my cruise. . . . I think, Mary, that you would make a splendid sailor, that is to say, if you were only a boy. I know that you would enjoy it. I intend to see every nook and corner of this little world, that is to be seen, if I live. I want to live on the sea, and die on the sea; and when once I set foot on a good ship as her commander I never want to leave her till I leave her a corpse. A ship at sea is a complete system in itself. The captain is king, and as absolute a monarch as ever lived. The officers are his house of lords, and some five hundred men his subjects. If a seaman is ordered to do an act, it must be done. The power of life and death is in the hands of the captain and his officers. One looks with as much pride and affection upon his ship as he would upon his wife. A man cannot be happier than when he is bowling along under a good breeze at fourteen knots an hour. And if you would see the sublime, I can imagine no place where sublimity lies more grand than in a storm at sea. I have stood on the Preble's deck [the *Preble* was an old sailing sloop of war used for practice cruises in the Chesapeake Bay] in such a storm that our old gray headed captain, who had been to sea since he was nine years old, said that he had never seen such a storm; and, at that time I would not have exchanged my post for the most brilliant place in the land. Such is life on the ocean, for those who have a taste for it. Of course, I do not speak of common seamen, for their life is at best a dog's life, but I had rather be an officer on board a man o' war than the President of les Etats-Unis.[11]

Early that June, Will and his classmates set sail on board the sailing sloop of war *Plymouth* for a cruise to Europe. The ship put in at Norfolk for repairs before crossing the Atlantic. The layover lasted several days and afforded Cushing the opportunity "to observe the F.F.V.s [First Families of Virginia]," as he put it in a letter to Cousin Mary. "I," he added, "like the renowned Yankee, failed, in spite of the most persevering, in finding one of the second families of that renowned old state."[12] While the *Plymouth* was being repaired, the midshipmen were housed on the ship of the line *Pennsylvania,* the largest U.S. warship ever built at that time, but relegated to duty as a receiving ship for new recruits. Cushing grew restless on the big old hulk, and one night after ten o'clock, he and several classmates broke into the shot lockers and began rolling cannon balls on the decks. The noise woke everyone up, and the pranksters were caught, but the punishment wasn't too severe.

During the Atlantic crossing, the ship survived a galley fire and weathered a storm. Cushing wasn't afraid of the storm, but reveled in its challenge, danger, and excitement. On July 17 the *Plymouth* anchored off the town of Horta on the island of Fayal in the Azores. The next morning Cushing and two shipmates went ashore and ordered dinner for six at a hotel to be ready by 3 P.M., then toured the island on the backs of mules.

The *Plymouth* returned home to find the country embroiled in crisis. The Compromise of 1850, the emergence of the Republican party, "bleeding Kansas," the Dred Scott case, and John Brown's raid on Harper's Ferry had driven wedges of separation between the North and the South. However you boil it down, at bottom lay the issue of slavery, with Northerners seeking to contain the "peculiar institution" and Southerners seeking to expand it. The crisis deepened after the election of "Honest Abe Lincoln, the Railsplitter," in November 1860. Slave owners feared that the "Black Republicans" meant to do away with slavery altogether. Debate raged in each Southern state as to whether to remain in the Union or to secede.

Inside the academy, the winter of 1860–61 was "a time of great suspense for all hands," as Robley Evans put it.[13] Many midshipmen remained moderate in expressing their sympathies. Northerners made rational arguments to convince Southerners to remain loyal. Southerners made equally rational arguments to justify secession. Neither side convinced the other. Some midshipmen tried to ignore current events, shunning discussions of slavery and secession in the hope that the storm would pass.

But the gathering storm was so big that it darkened the entire nation, including the academy. Many a Southerner voiced his allegiance to his state and to the Confederacy, while many a Northerner voiced his allegiance to the Union. Some Southerners took to wearing secession badges on their uniforms. A middie from North Carolina told Alfred Thayer Mahan that James Buchanan would be the last President of the United States. Fistfights between Northern and Southern midshipmen became increasingly common. One day at the height of the crisis, a group of Southerners was discussing the sympathies of the citizens of Baltimore. William T. Sampson, honor man of 1861, was passing by. Their words stopped him in his tracks. "You say if the capital of the nation is attacked," Sampson said slowly, his voice rising, "Northern troops will not be permitted to march through Baltimore to protect it? Well then," he nearly shouted, "the North will march over Baltimore—or the place where it stood!"[14]

Cushing stood ready to die for the North. "Political affairs look decidedly squally at present," he wrote Cousin Mary from Annapolis on December 12, 1860.

> Even here, in Maryland, there is a terrible excitement. Men are arming in every portion of the state; all the banks have suspended; and the blue cockade may be seen in every nook and corner. Within the Academy, where there are representatives from every state in our Union, the huge weight of the crisis has penetrated. Midn. are every day resigning. Every Southerner has orders to resign as soon as their states secede. Secession speeches are made by the South Carolinians and Georgians, and there is not a Southern man but hopes and believes that the world now views for the last time this great Republic.
>
> There is no money in the treasury; the U.S. officers can not be paid; and even if Congress does issue treasury notes, no one will take them. Here a government check is not worth five cents to the dollar. I have seen them repeatedly refused. Matters can not be improved except by a miracle; and unless that miracle happens, the ship of State, which has been so long on a lee shore, must go down, carrying with it the Naval Academy, which is but a speck on its deck. . . .
>
> But if it comes to blows between the North and South, I will shed the last drop of my blood for the state of New York. If this place does break up, I will get my graduating papers. If it does not, I will get them all the same, but in one case it will be in June, and in the other it will be—Well! may be, in less than a month.[15]

Although Cushing never considered any course but loyalty to the Union, he did share certain sentiments with Southerners. Like most white Americans of that era, he harbored the attitude that had made slavery possible—racism, the belief that the black race was inherently inferior to the white race. In correspondence with Cousin Mary, Cushing referred to an African American they both knew as "a great darkey" and "a lump of darkness."[16] Once when transporting a heavy trunk full of Fredonia produce from Baltimore to Annapolis, a local tough asked him what it contained. Cushing joked that he was selling a black man south. "I affirmed that I was running off with a gentleman of dark complexion," as he put it to Cousin Mary.[17] And while Cushing stood ready to fight to preserve the Union, he felt that honor demanded that the Southern states should secede. "I believe that the South has been deeply wronged," he wrote his cousin on December 12, "and that unless it can procure security for the safety of its slave property; that it would be cowardly for it to stay in the union."[18]

South Carolina in fact seceded five days later. "This will probably be the new 4th of July for a Southern Confederacy," Cushing wrote Cousin Mary.[19]

Although Cushing's Yankee blood boiled when Southern sympathizers voiced or otherwise displayed their sentiments, he didn't take current events so seriously that he couldn't view them with a little sarcasm. Volunteers for the Southern cause frequently paraded through town during the winter of 1860–61. "I can see from my windows, a barbarian from the 'Eastern Shore,' calling himself, I believe a Zouave," Cushing wrote Cousin Mary on December 17. "He is clad just at present in smiles and red flannel. The latter intending to represent by its color, I suppose, the blood of thousands of Northerners, to be slain in time to come. I tremble as I write!"[20]

In another letter to Cousin Mary he managed to fling a few barbs at his hometown as well as at secession. "I get all the (public) village news from the 'Advertiser' and 'Censor,'" he wrote of the Fredonia newspapers.

What amuses me the most in them is the way that they speak of the political issues of the day. The South can hold its own against [New York City newspapers] the 'Times' and 'Tribune' but if I were to let it be known that the 'Fredonia Censor' threatens the rebellious states with chastisement, I doubt not that there would be fear and trembling in Southern homes.[21]

Cushing had expressed negative thoughts about Fredonia before. "I am never going back to Fredonia," he had written Cousin Mary the previous spring.

There are very few persons there whom I wish to see; and if I have any influence with mother she will never spend another spring in that village. I am going to have Milton escort mother to Boston next April, and in four years, when I am a lieutenant, I am going to find some nice place down south, and when I am ashore, make that my home. . . . I would like to travel through Wisconsin: you know it is my native state. I have not been in the state since I was four years old.

In a letter to his sister Mary written in 1864, Cushing referred to the people of Fredonia as "idiots."[22]

Cushing's denigration of Fredonia reflected a sense of embarrassment at his own social stature. While his father had been alive, particularly while the family lived in the near wilds of Wisconsin, they had been big fish in a small pond because of Milton's medical degree and stature as justice of the peace and chairman of Prairieville's board of supervisors. Even in Chicago, home to some gigantic critters, Milton's thriving medical practice kept the family swimming ahead of most of the small fry in town, socioeconomically speaking. But in Fredonia, with Milton dead and the family dependent on Mary Cushing in a society that considered women inferior to men, the family's social status fell a few notches. Although Will had always had a macho streak a mile wide, doubtless developed to compensate for his position as the youngest brother, after his father died, he used machismo to compensate for his reduced size in the pond, psychologically speaking.

Will Cushing's machismo, born of a need to crush his own sense of inadequacy, fostered in him strong resentment of people who considered themselves socially superior to others. The crisis of the Union zeroed Cushing's resentment in on members of the Southern aristocracy who considered themselves better than most people. Cushing's response to the "chivalry,"[23] as he called them, was intense patriotism.

Cushing's patriotism surfaced frequently in his letters. On December 22, 1860, for example, he sent Cousin Mary some photographs of the academy, including one of the battery. "The 'stars and stripes' still wave over it," he wrote. "Thank God!!"[24]

Outside the academy, tensions ran high as nobody could yet say which side Maryland would choose. If the state joined the Confederacy, the federal government risked losing the academy's guns and ammunition. This prospect turned the naval school into an armed camp, with armed sentries guarding her gates.

Meanwhile, against the backdrop of impending national catastrophe, a personal drama began to unfold for Cushing. Even during the winter of 1860–61, the crisis of the Union didn't occupy midshipmen's every waking moment. There were still classes to attend, meals to eat, and the myriad other things to do that comprised their day-to-day lives. Plenty of opportunities remained for Cushing's temper and mile-wide mischievous streak to surface. These traits nearly shipwrecked his naval career.

Throughout his first-class year, as senior year was and is called at the academy, Cushing was as cocky as ever. He had become careless in his dress, he still spent a large portion of his study hours visiting friends instead of hitting the books, and he never developed that awe of the superior officer that martinets find so gratifying. Nevertheless, he did reasonably well in academics and, midway through the year, he stood sixth in ethics, seventh in gunnery, ninth in artillery, eleventh in philosophy, twenty-fifth in modern languages, and sixth in general order of merit in a class of twenty-seven members. The fact that Cushing did so well despite putting forth so little effort must have rankled the martinets.

Cushing began the new year of 1861 by butting heads with the academy's top-ranking officer. Capt. George S. Blake held that position longer than any other superintendent in academy history—eight years. Blake claimed to have never wronged a midshipman, took a fatherly interest in them, and personally answered more than a thousand letters a year from their parents. By all accounts he was well liked.

You would think that Cushing would have had to work pretty hard to anger such a man, but he managed to do it rather easily. Early that January, Cushing obtained leave to care for a favorite aunt who was confined to bed by illness and all alone in a hotel in Washington. The superintendent assumed the aunt in question was the wife of Commodore Smith. When he asked the commodore about his wife, Smith said she was fine. When Cushing returned to Annapolis, the superintendent charged him with lying. The charge infuriated Cushing. Losing his temper, the midshipman called the superintendent a liar. When he discovered he had the wrong aunt, the superintendent dropped the charge, but he didn't forget Cushing's lapse in deference.

Cushing, meanwhile, had been up to his old tricks, breaking the rules to relieve the boredom of what later generations of midshipmen called the "dark ages," that seemingly interminable stretch between Christmas and the onset of spring. By February Cushing had racked up 147 demerits for his first-class year.

Throughout the year, Cushing had been at odds with his Spanish professor, a dignified and dapper man named Edward A. Roget. The professor's colleagues considered him a gentleman and an excellent scholar, but many midshipmen saw him as an effeminate dandy and referred to him as "the Don." True to his nature, Cushing didn't conceal his disdain for the professor, often mimicking him to the delight of his classmates.

Emboldened by getting away with small acts of rebellion, Cushing's behavior toward the Don grew more and more outrageous. Once Roget dressed in his best suit to meet a young lady. Cushing set a bucket of water atop the doorway through which the professor had to pass to greet his date. The dousing humiliated and enraged the professor. Roget suspected Cushing, but could prove nothing, so Cushing got away with the prank.

But Cushing pressed his luck once too often. On January 14, 1861 Roget had the misfortune of crossing a street in Annapolis in front of a vicious cart horse. The animal expressed its displeasure at the professor's audacity by biting him severely on the shoulder. News of the incident delighted Cushing and inspired him to sketch a cartoon on the flyleaf of his Spanish textbook. The cartoon depicted Roget in the act of biting the horse's neck. "The poor old Don," said the caption, "he bit the hoss!"

When Roget appeared in class the next day with his shoulder swathed in bandages, he found the students gathered around Cushing's desk, snickering at his textbook. Perhaps wearing a smile, he wondered what was so funny and asked to see the book. The smile vanished when he saw the cartoon and realized they were laughing at him. "I did not bite the horse!" he shouted angrily. "The horse bit me!"[25]

Roget's outburst only increased the midshipmen's merriment. When the class had nearly quieted, he ruined the moment himself by muttering that it was absurd for anyone to think he would bite the neck of a horse. The comment plunged the midshipmen into convulsions of laughter. After class Roget stormed over to the superintendent's house and demanded Cushing's immediate dismissal. The superintendent, of course, refused, for he couldn't dismiss a midshipman without due process.

But Roget soon had his revenge. The next month, Cushing failed the Spanish exam. In a tersely worded report to the Navy Department, the superintendent recommended Cushing's dismissal. "Deficient at February semi-annual examination, 1861. Midshipman William B. Cushing. Deficient in Spanish," it said. "Aptitude for study: good. Habits of study: irregular. General conduct: bad. Aptitude for Naval Service: not good. Not recommended for continuance at the Academy."[26] On March 23, 1861, just three months shy of graduation, Cushing was "returned to his friends," to use the old euphemism.

It was up to secretary of the Navy Gideon Welles to inform the young man of the final decision regarding his dismissal. "Saddened disappointment and grief," Welles later recalled, "shadowed his juvenile face."[27]

The circumstances of his ouster were somewhat shady. "It certainly was an unusual proceeding to dismiss a first classman, standing high in his class, for being unsatisfactory in Spanish," his quasi-official biographer Charles Stewart wrote. "One is forced to conclude that some personal resentment entered largely into the motives for prompting summary action in his case."[28]

Cushing left Annapolis for Washington and stayed in the home of Commodore Smith. While wandering the streets, he ran into several classmates who had resigned and were passing through the capital on their way south to join the Confederate navy. They suggested that Cushing join them in rebellion against the federal government. Cushing refused, placing loyalty to his country above his hurt feelings. Cushing also ran into one of his instructors from the academy, Lt. Charles W. Flusser. Cushing had developed a deep and abiding respect for Flusser, whom he later recalled as "a man of clearest judgement, lion-like bravery, and a pure patriotism."[29] The lieutenant, a Maryland native and Kentucky resident, was wrestling with the dilemma of which side to join. Cushing convinced him to remain loyal to the U.S. flag.

News of the Confederate attack on Fort Sumter inflamed Cushing's patriotic spirit. He marched over to the Navy Department, called on Gideon Welles, and asked for a place, any place, in the Navy.

Welles pondered Cushing's case over the next several days. On the one hand, George Blake and another prominent officer had declared that Cushing was "inattentive to certain studies," "boyish and wayward," and "wanting in essential elements which were requisite to the make-up of a good Naval Officer." On the other hand, several prominent officers had spoken favorably about the young man. Flusser put in a good word for Cushing with Maj. Gen. Benjamin F. Butler, then in command of Army forces at Annapolis. Butler, in turn, brought Cushing's case to the attention of Gustavus V. Fox, who had been his roommate at Bowdoin College and was now Assistant Secretary of the Navy. Joseph Smith also spoke out on Cushing's behalf. The young man's problems at the academy were "scholastic rather than naval," declared the old commodore, "not essential to his profession, and wholly insufficient" to justify his dismissal.[30]

Gideon Welles was an uncannily good judge of character. He decided to give Cushing another chance. "Sympathy for the youth, whose perseverance, enthusiasm and zeal impressed me," he recalled years later, "had probably as much influence as the recommendations of his friends." Welles summoned the young man into his office and gave him the good news. Grateful for the opportunity, Cushing said, as Welles recalled, that "I should never have cause to regret his re-instatement in the service."[31] In an appointment backdated to April 1, Welles made Cushing an acting volunteer master's mate and assigned him to the USS *Minnesota.*

Chapter 3

Rough Ride to Renown

WITH HIS COMMISSION in hand, Cushing began his climb through the naval officer ranks to a position from which he could launch an assault on the summit of everlasting fame. It was a tricky ascent, however, with misstep often following step, as Cushing alternated between daring feat and faux pas, both of which came naturally to a man with his courage and contempt for those whom he considered lacking.

The United States Navy that Cushing had just reentered was like a dry sponge thrust into a bucket of water. In April 1861 the fleet consisted of forty-two operational vessels. Most of them were overseas on foreign stations or in the Gulf of Mexico. Only three warships were available immediately for service on the Atlantic coast. Fortunately for the Union, Gideon Welles was an outstanding administrator as well as a keen judge of character. Together with the energetic Gustavus Fox, Welles launched an unprecedented expansion of the Navy. By the end of 1861, the fleet had swelled to 264 vessels. By the end of the war, the U.S. Navy—which Civil War historians refer to as the Union Navy—had peaked at more than 650 ships.

While Gideon Welles was considering whether or not to offer Cushing a commission, Abraham Lincoln was considering how to use the Navy against the rebellion. After the surrender of Fort Sumter, Confederate president Jefferson Davis called for entrepreneurs to outfit privateers to prey on Northern commerce, a move characteristic of weaker naval powers during the nineteenth century. Abraham Lincoln retaliated by proclaiming a blockade of the states that had seceded. The blockade became the Navy's principal mission during the war.

At first, the Union Navy deployed only one squadron to cover the thousand miles of coastline from Alexandria, Virginia, to Key West, Florida. In September 1861, the Navy Department divided this command in two, forming the North Atlantic Blockading Squadron and the South Atlantic Blockading Squadron. The area of responsibility for the North Atlantic Blockading Squadron stretched from the Chesapeake Bay to the North Carolina–South Carolina border and included the coastal and inland waters of Virginia and North Carolina.

Cushing served in the North Atlantic Blockading Squadron throughout the war. The steam frigate *Minnesota* to which he had been assigned was the flagship. The *Minnesota* represented the cream of the antebellum Navy. She had gone to sea in 1857 as one of the U.S. Navy's largest and most powerful warships, arguably the best of the *Merrimack* class. The heavy, deep-draft, wooden-hulled frigate measured almost 265 feet at the waterline, displaced 4,833 tons, could make 12.5 knots, and carried 52 guns and more than 500 officers and men.

April 1861 found the *Minnesota* in the Boston Navy Yard undergoing extensive repairs. Cushing arrived in Boston toward the end of the month. The *Minnesota* departed from Boston on May 7, bound for Hampton Roads, Virginia. Cushing, one of the four most junior officers on board, was placed in charge of the berth deck, where the sailors slung their hammocks. It was, he noted later in life with characteristic sarcasm, "the lowest of all positions in a man o' war."[1]

At the time, however, Cushing was elated to be serving on a

big ship going off to war. "I am an officer on board the splendid steam frigate Minnesota," he wrote Cousin Mary on the day the ship set sail.

> I am going to fight under the old banner of freedom. I may never return, but if I die it shall be under the folds of the flag that sheltered my infancy, and while striking a blow for its honor, and my own. . . . Wherever there is fighting there we will be, and where there is danger in the battle there I will be, for I will gain a name in this war.[2]

The *Minnesota* arrived at Hampton Roads after a quiet passage of six days. Hampton Roads remained of vital strategic significance throughout the war. Three Virginia rivers, the James, Nansemond, and Elizabeth, emptied into Hampton Roads through its eastern and southern entrances. The western entrance of Hampton Roads linked these rivers to the Chesapeake Bay. Canals connected the Nansemond and Elizabeth Rivers to North Carolina. Thus, one flotilla of blockaders operating in Hampton Roads severely pinched off the maritime commerce between the outside world and the region drained by these rivers, particularly the Confederate capital, Richmond, which lay up the James.

Two spits of land thrust into Hampton Roads from above and below at the juncture with the Chesapeake Bay. At the tip of the northern spit lay seventy-five acres of federal property known as Old Point Comfort. On this land stood Fort Monroe. Dubbed the "Gibraltar of the Chesapeake," Fort Monroe boasted seven thirty-five-foot-high granite walls. Its heavy guns commanded the channel into the Chesapeake from the north. Conceived in the wake of British depredations during the War of 1812, the fort had emerged in the 1830s as the strongest link in America's chain of coastal fortifications. Unlike Fort Sumter, it remained in Union hands and a thorn in the side of the Confederacy throughout the Civil War. Union leaders soon transformed it into a bastion for the Army and an important logistical base for the Navy.

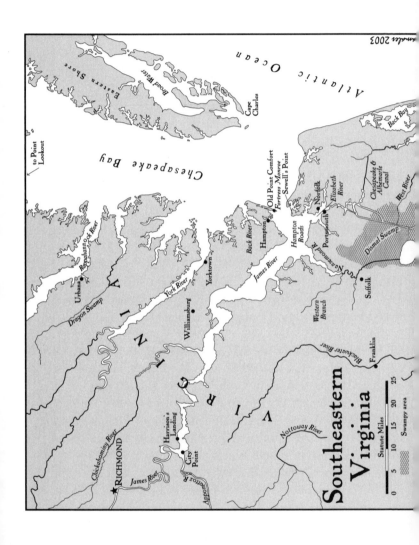

Southeastern Virginia

Statute Miles

0   5   10   15   20   25

Swampy area

Atlantic Ocean

Chesapeake Bay

Eastern Shore

Broad Water

Cape Charles

to Point Lookout

Rappahannock River

Urbanna

Dragon Swamp

York River

Yorktown

Williamsburg

VIRGINIA

RICHMOND ★

Chickahominy River

James River

Harrison's Landing

City Point

Appomattox R.

Nottoway River

Back River

Hampton

Fortress Monroe

Old Point Comfort

Sewell's Point

Hampton Roads

Norfolk

Elizabeth River

Portsmouth

Nansemond R.

Western Branch

Suffolk

Blackwater River

Franklin

Dismal Swamp

Chesapeake & Albemarle Canal

West River

Back Bay

smith 2003

At Hampton Roads, the *Minnesota* joined forces with the sailing sloop *Cumberland,* the screw steamer *Monticello,* and the side-wheeler *Quaker City.* Blockaders were assigned patrol stations off of various Southern ports, inlets, and river mouths. When a blockader sighted a vessel in its patrol area, it chased the vessel down, stopped it, and sent over a boarding party. The officer in charge of the boarding party inspected the ship's bill of lading, register, cargo manifest, invoices, and charter. If the papers checked out and the officer deemed the vessel innocent of breaking any law, he allowed her to proceed. If something in the papers made the officer suspicious of an infraction or if the vessel was obviously carrying contraband cargo, the vessel became a lawful prize of war. The blockader put a prize crew on board, and the crew took the vessel into a Northern port, where a federal prize court adjudicated the case. If the court found the vessel innocent, she was released. If not, the vessel and her cargo were condemned and sold and, after adjudication costs were paid, half the proceeds went to the Navy pension fund and the other half was divided in proportion to their pay among the men of the blockader or blockaders that captured her.

The squadron soon captured its first prizes. Flag Officer Silas Stringham, the squadron commander, was short of junior officers and assigned Cushing to take one of the three prizes, the schooner *Delaware Farmer,* to Philadelphia in command of the original crew. The schooner arrived in Philadelphia amidst much fanfare for she was the first prize brought into that port. Although Cushing received a hero's welcome, he received no prize money, for the ship's owner argued successfully in court that the Navy had seized the vessel illegally.

When Cushing rejoined the squadron, Flag Officer Stringham gave him another prize, the bark *Pioneer,* a Southern-owned ship with a Southern crew. Cushing was to take the bark to New York. Because of the shortage of manpower, Stringham could spare only one other officer to accompany him. Armed with revolvers, Cushing and the other officer stood watch over the sixteen-man crew throughout the voyage to New York. Cushing reveled in the challenge. He wrote his mother as the *Pioneer* sailed north:

> I feel the weight of a brace of revolvers on my belt, and I know not at what moment the crew may try to retake her; but your boy is ready, and I trust no son of yours is a coward. Now I must go and have the pumps sounded in order to see that none of the crew have scuttled her.[3]

The *Pioneer* arrived in New York without incident. When Cushing and the other officer returned to Hampton Roads, Stringham commended them, for he realized how dangerous the mission they had just accomplished had been.

Cushing commended himself as well. "In the short time that the blockade has been established," he wrote Cousin Mary on June 25, "I have been on active service in the South, and I have been to the North twice in command of valuable prize ships captured from the enemy. . . . I have gained considerable honor by taking them in, safely, to New York and Philadelphia, and I expect promotion before long.[4]

Blockade duty entailed far more than chasing blockade-runners on the high seas. The crews of ships operating in bays, sounds, and rivers were in almost daily contact with civilians or enemy forces afloat or ashore. Such contact variously involved enemy snipers plinking at ships; ships stopping and inspecting commercial traffic, small boats, and, indeed, anything that floated; ships stopping for bumboats, whose wares augmented the hearty but bland sailors' diet, and whose occupants were known to sell alcohol in cans marked "oysters"; boat parties hunting or foraging ashore; boat parties running into cavalry while hunting or foraging ashore; boat parties making forays ashore to attack guerrillas or raid cattle or burn saltworks or cut out Southerners' boats; and a thousand other variations on the theme of up-close-and-personal contact with the enemy. It was in these types of operations that Cushing came to excel.

Cushing embarked on the first such mission in July 1861. Maj. Gen. Ben Butler, now commander of the Union Army's Depart-

Midshipman William B. Cushing, age 14, c. 1857.
Historical Museum of the D. R. Barker Library

Lt. William B. Cushing, U.S. Navy, c. 1864.
Library of Congress

Lt. Comdr. Charles W. Flusser, U.S. Navy. Engraving published in William Henry Powell. *Officers of the Army and Navy (Regular) Who Served in the Civil War.* Philadelphia: J. B. Lippincott, 1892

Rear Adm. Samuel Phillips Lee, U.S. Navy. *Carte de visite,* c. 1863.
Library of Congress

USS *Commodore Barney.*
Library of Congress

CSS *Albemarle*, by R. G. Skerrett, 1899. Sepia wash drawing.
Naval Historical Center

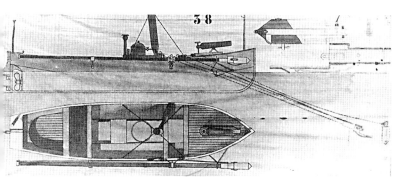

Picket Boat No. 1, from original plans, 1864.
Naval Historical Center

Picket Boat No. 1 underway. Engraving after a painting by R. G. Skerrett, 1900.
Naval Historical Center

Rear Adm. David Dixon Porter, U.S. Navy, c. 1863.
Naval Historical Center

Destruction of the CSS *Albemarle*. Engraving after a drawing by
Julian Oliver Davidson, c. 1885.
National Archives

Lt. Cmdr. William B. Cushing (left) with Rear Adm. David Dixon Porter (center) and his staff on board the USS *Malvern* at Hampton Roads, December 1864. Lt. Samuel W. Preston stands second from right and Acting Ens. John W. Grattan is at the far right.
Library of Congress

Lt. Benjamin H. Porter, U.S. Navy, c. 1864.
Naval Historical Center

ASSAULT OF THE NAVAL COLUMN ON THE NORTH-EAST SALIENT OF FORT FISHER.

Sailors attempting to "board" Fort Fisher.
Naval Historical Center

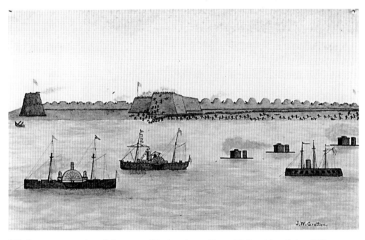

High watermark of the naval brigade at Fort Fisher, by John W. Grattan, n.d. Watercolor. The USS *Malvern*, second from left, flies signal flags. To the right are three monitors and the USS *New Ironsides. Naval Historical Center*

Katharine Louise (Forbes) Cushing.
Historical Museum of the D. R. Barker Library

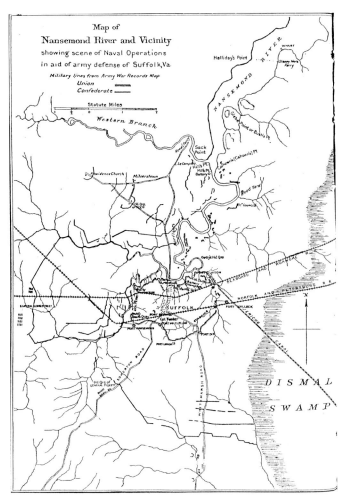

Nansemond River and vicinity.
United States Naval Institute Proceedings 38 (June 1912)

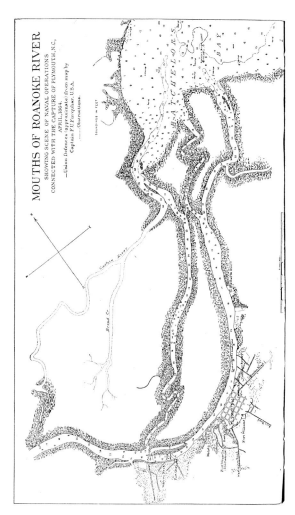

Mouths of Roanoke River.
United States Naval Institute Proceedings 38 (June 1912)

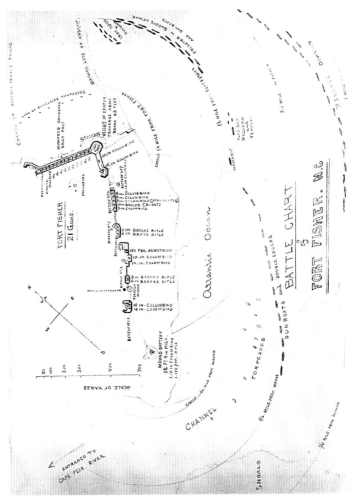

Battle chart of Fort Fisher, by John W. Grattan, c. 1865.
Library of Congress

ment of Virginia, had reported a Rebel buildup along the Back River and had requested Flag Officer Stringham to mount a raid. When Cushing heard of the mission, he volunteered immediately. On July 24, five launches full of sailors under the command of Lt. Pierce Crosby joined four launches full of soldiers from Fort Monroe and headed upriver. They burned ten small schooners and sloops and captured a schooner "heavily loaded with corn, provisions, and other articles," noted Stringham in his report to Gideon Welles. "They discovered no batteries or any body of Rebels, seeing occasional scouts. They met with no accident."[5]

Although the raid was a success, Cushing was disappointed that there had been no fighting. He put the best face on his first mission behind enemy lines in a letter to Cousin Mary. "I have been in action," he declared, "have burned my first powder in anger and have felt the leaden bullet whiz by my head on its deadly mission."[6]

The raid, the July heat, or something else may have given Cushing a premonition of his brother's death.

> I may resign before long, and go into the land service . . . I have no doubt but that I can procure a captain's birth [sic] in the volunteers. I so long to be near Allie. It seems as if I might be some protection to him in the time of action. If the Rebels should kill him, I don't think that I would be a man any longer. I should become a fiend. I love that boy better than I do my own life: and I would not live without my brother. For myself, I care nothing. I am drifting about the world with every wind and tide. I take my fate with me, and whate'r it may be, I hope to meet it like a man.[7]

Cushing's machismo nearly nipped his promising naval career in the bud. For some time he had not been getting along with a superior officer on the *Minnesota*. By mid-August their relationship had degenerated to the point that Cushing felt he had to risk his life to protect his honor. He submitted a letter of resignation from the Navy, as he told Cousin Mary, "for the purpose of challenging a superior officer. The rule is that if a superior is challenged by his inferior he is not honor bound to accept the challenge. So in order to gain my end I was forced to resign."[8] Cushing didn't say who the superior was or why he felt his honor had been so violated that it called for a duel. Biographer Charles Stewart mentioned a lieutenant who "had been particularly offensive to Cushing and had lorded it over his junior officers,"[9] so it is easy to imagine that the lieutenant insulted Cushing, who threw down the gauntlet in reply.

Flag Officer Stringham didn't have time to consider Cushing's resignation, for he was busy preparing a joint expedition against Hatteras Inlet on the North Carolina coast. Confederate privateers and warships of the North Carolina Navy had been grabbing so many prizes off Cape Hatteras that Gideon Welles came to consider the area a "pirate's nest." In the summer of 1861, he devised a plan to eliminate this threat by sending an expedition to plug up Oregon Inlet, Hatteras Inlet, and Ocracoke Inlet, through which ships operating from the ports dotting Albemarle Sound, Pamlico Sound, and the rivers emptying into them passed into the Atlantic. On August 26, the *Minnesota,* her sister ship the *Wabash,* three smaller steam warships, and the sailing sloop *Cumberland* under Flag Officer Stringham set sail for Hatteras Inlet along with two Army transports carrying some 860 troops under General Butler.

Forts Hatteras and Clark, two small Confederate sand-and-log forts built on the northern headland and mounting a total of fifteen guns, guarded the inlet. Stringham intended to bombard the forts with his heavier ships while the three smaller steamers covered a landing by Butler's troops a few miles up from the northernmost fort, Fort Clark. Once the Navy had softened up the forts, the Army was to march in and administer the coup de grâce. Cushing, in command of the flagship's quarterdeck division of 8-inch shell guns, stood in a position that enabled him to see the entire battle unfold.

The Union fleet opened fire on Fort Clark at about ten o'clock on August 28. The Rebels returned fire almost immediately. "This was a great moment for me," Cushing later recalled.

"I shall never forget or again experience the wild pleasure and excitement that I felt."[10] Shots from the fort fell short or flew over the ships, while the Navy gunners soon found their mark.

Cushing couldn't help but notice the excitement and brave demeanor of Flag Officer Stringham. "I remember well our gallant old captain's look as the first whiz of Rebel iron came to our ears," Cushing wrote in his memoirs. "With flushed face and sparkling eye he straightened his tall form, and with gray hair bared to the sun, stamped his foot upon the bridge and impulsively exclaimed 'Glorious! glorious—closer! closer!' "[11]

Shortly after noon the Confederate flag over Fort Clark came down, and the fort's defenders fled toward Fort Hatteras. The fleet bombarded Fort Hatteras for the rest of that afternoon. The next morning the ships opened fire at 8 A.M. Just over three hours later, the Confederates inside Fort Hatteras raised a white flag. "With no casualty of any consequence whatever," as the skipper of one of the troop transports reported to Gideon Welles, Union forces captured two forts, 715 prisoners, and kicked in the door to eastern North Carolina.[12] It was a lopsided victory, the Navy's first in the war.

Some time after the gun smoke had cleared, Cushing began referring to Flag Officer Stringham as "Old Sting 'em."[13] The flag officer soon caught wind of the nickname, but the admiration inherent in it was lost on him. Although Cushing had intended it as a compliment, the nickname turned out to be a devastating faux pas, for to Stringham it smacked of insubordination.

In mid-September, Flag Officer Stringham forwarded Cushing's resignation to Gustavus Fox and recommended that Fox accept it. Cushing's "visionary and speculative turn of mind," Stringham wrote, "makes him unfit for the naval service."[14] The Navy Department did so. Cushing was out of the Navy.

Cushing immediately tried to get back in. Whether or not he remained intent on the duel he had mentioned to Cousin Mary, he sought reinstatement as a midshipman in the class of 1861 at the end of September. He wrote to Flag Officer Stringham, asking him to "state in writing whether I did my duty while under your command," particularly "when I went north in prize vessels" and when "I had command of the quarter-deck division of guns, immediately under your eye" at the battle of Hatteras Inlet. Stringham sent a terse reply, referring Cushing to the *Minnesota*'s skipper, "as you were more immediately under his command." "As regards the times that you refer to," Stringham added begrudgingly, "I am happy to say your conduct was meritorious."[15]

Once again, Gideon Welles sat down to ponder Cushing's future in the Navy. Stringham, as Welles later recalled, thought Cushing "too full of levity, too fond of fun and frolic to make a valuable officer." But Welles sensed that Cushing was, in fact, bored with his role as a junior officer on the flagship. "The truth was," Welles noted, "with his exuberant spirit he had too little to do; his restless, active mind was filled with adventure and zeal to accomplish something that would do himself credit and the country service."[16]

But Welles needed more than a gut feeling to justify reinstating Cushing, so he wrote to the superintendent of the Naval Academy. George Blake had had a change of heart about the lad.

> In my opinion, the abilities of that young gentleman are very good. But while at the Naval Academy he was at times very idle and insubordinate and his failure in his studies was due to the former course alone. I am certain, however, that he can become a good officer, and as his services on board the Minnesota have been satisfactory to the Department, I respectfully suggest that he be restored.[17]

It wasn't exactly a ringing endorsement, but it would do.

Meanwhile, Cushing went to Washington to await Welles's decision. Allie was in Washington too, fresh from the front lines in Virginia. After graduating from West Point on June 24, 1861, Allie was commissioned a second lieutenant in the Fourth United States Artillery, got his baptism by fire at Bull Run, and spent the remainder of the summer drilling and fortifying the capital. By the time Will arrived in September, Allie had been promoted to the temporary rank of captain.

Shortly after Will got there, so did a letter from Cousin Mary, asking him to be best man in her wedding. Will wished her well, but declined the invitation, perhaps embarrassed by the uncertainty of his future in the Navy.

The waiting ended on October 19, when Welles reinstated Cushing as a midshipman in the class of 1861, giving him the same rank as if he had graduated on time with his classmates. Welles ordered him back to the North Atlantic Blockading Squadron to serve on board the gunboat *Cambridge*, a small screw-propelled former merchant steamer. The *Cambridge* was considerably lower on the naval totem pole than the lofty, majestic *Minnesota,* but she could operate in much shallower water, which made her a much more suitable platform from which to launch raids behind enemy lines. In early November the *Cambridge* arrived at her blockading station off the mouth of the Rappahannock River. The first few days were quiet enough to enable the crew to do some duck hunting and oystering.

Soon an opportunity arose for action. On October 31, a group of slaves, numbering more than thirty, escaped from their Virginia owners, took a boat, and rowed out to the *Cambridge.* They told Comdr. William A. Parker, the skipper, of a schooner loaded with wheat and wood anchored some five or six miles up the Corrotoman Creek, a tributary of the Rappahannock. Commander Parker immediately began planning a cutting out expedition. Cushing volunteered to go.

On November 6, a detachment of thirty men from the *Cambridge* under the command of Lt. William Gwin, assisted by two acting masters and Cushing, the most junior officer, set out on board the steam tug *Rescue* to capture or burn the schooner. The Yankee sailors proceeded up the creek without incident and found the schooner hard aground. After spending about two hours trying to free the schooner, they set her afire along with a large pile of wood on shore.

On the way back down, more than one hundred Rebel soldiers, concealed by thick underbrush on both sides of the creek, opened up on the tug with small arms and a rifled cannon. The

Yankee sailors returned fire with Sharps rifles and the *Rescue's* 32-pounder. Cushing was in charge of the cannon. "The first round of canister that I fired swept nearly every man from their gun," he later boasted. He then turned the 32-pounder on a house in which dozens of Confederate riflemen were holed up and fired a shell that tore the house to pieces and reportedly killed a number of soldiers. The Rebels botched the ambush, for they didn't manage to hit any Yankees, except for one spent musket ball that struck one of the officers. In a letter to Cousin Mary, Cushing described the action as though he were in command. He said that a splinter torn from the tug by one of the Rebel cannon balls ripped his jacket. After the firefight, the splinter was found "reposing safely upon my breast." [18]

While on patrol in rivers, the mission of Union warships included eliminating threats to friendly shipping and denying the enemy access to the waterways. On November 8 the *Cambridge* bombarded the town of Urbana on the banks of the Rappahannock. Escaped slaves had reported that the Rebels had a storehouse of ammunition in the town, guarded by soldiers in a nearby encampment. The *Cambridge* drove off the defenders, and the crew cut out the town's mail boat. The next day, the *Cambridge* shelled two points on shore where the "Chivalry," as Cushing was given to calling the Rebels, had been putting up batteries to challenge Union control of the Rappahannock. The guns had not yet been mounted, and the *Cambridge* destroyed the emplacements. For the next few days the ship steamed thirty or forty miles upriver, then down again, back and forth, to draw Rebel fire so that they could locate and destroy any masked Rebel batteries. The *Cambridge* had no further encounters with the enemy. In a month, more than four hundred "imps of darkness," as Cushing sometimes called runaway slaves, escaped to the *Cambridge.*[19] Commander Parker sent them on to Fort Monroe.

The *Cambridge* spent the winter off the Virginia capes, intercepting commerce in search of blockade violators. Cushing led many a boarding party during these months. "I was frequently out in open boats for five and six hours at a time with the icy seas and sleet dashing over me continually," he wrote in his memoirs. "Several times I was too stiff upon return to step over the ship's side and had to be hoisted on deck."[20] The exposure took its toll on Cushing's health.

On March 8, 1862 the *Cambridge* was off of Hampton Roads on blockade duty in company with the sailing ships *Congress, Cumberland,* and *St. Lawrence,* the steam frigate *Minnesota* and her sister ship *Roanoke,* and several tugs. For months the Union Navy had been monitoring reports that the Confederates were converting the wreck of the steam frigate *Merrimack* into an ironclad warship at the Gosport navy yard across the Elizabeth River from Norfolk. At about one o'clock that afternoon, lookouts signaled that the Confederate ironclad was coming down.

The *Merrimack,* sister ship of the *Minnesota,* had been the first of her class to go to sea. Her poor engines condemned her to a fiery death and a watery grave when Union forces evacuated Norfolk in April 1861. In keeping with their initial strategy to beat the Union navy with technologically superior armored warships, the Confederates resurrected the *Merrimack,* converted her into an ironclad, and renamed her the *Virginia.*

The *Virginia* made straight for the *Cumberland,* rammed her, and sank her. The crew of the *Cumberland* fought back with incredible bravery, but the shot from their guns just bounced off the ironclad's sloped armor "like India-rubber balls," as the *Cumberland's* pilot put it.[21] The *Virginia* next went after the *Congress,* which had grounded while trying to move out of range. Gunfire from the Confederate ironclad set the sitting duck on fire. As the day drew to a close, the *Virginia* traded shots with the *Minnesota,* which had run aground while trying to intercept the ironclad.

When the *Virginia* first appeared, the *Cambridge* steamed out to the *St. Lawrence,* some five miles from the scene of the action, took her in tow, and, at about 2:30, started for Hampton Roads. At 5:25, when the pair came abreast of the Confederate batteries on Sewell's Point, gunners on the ships and on shore fired a few rounds at one another. A few Rebel rounds struck the *Cam-*

bridge, but did no appreciable damage. At 5:50 the *St. Lawrence* grounded near the *Minnesota* while Cushing's old ship was trading shots with the *Virginia.* The sailing frigate fired a few rounds at the *Virginia,* but these, too, bounced off. In return, the *Virginia* planted a shell deep inside the *St. Lawrence,* but fortunately for the frigate, the shell didn't explode. Another shell from the *Virginia* exploded above the deck of the *Cambridge,* wounding Cushing's hand. The *Cambridge* struggled for two hours to get the *St. Lawrence* afloat. A tug finally managed to free the sailing ship, and the *Cambridge* towed her to Fort Monroe. That night Cushing wrote a letter to his mother, expressing pride in being the only officer wounded on his ship and claiming that the gun he was in command of shot away the Rebel flagstaff on Sewell's Point.

That evening a strange apparition appeared in Hampton Roads. It proved to be the USS *Monitor,* her way lit by the still-burning *Congress.* Of a far more radical design than the Rebel ironclad, the *Monitor* featured a low, iron hull topped by a revolving turret that mounted two guns.

As Cushing put it in his memoirs, March 9 was "a day, big with the fate of future navies!" When "the Rebel monster" reappeared that morning to finish off the wooden blockaders, "a black speck" stood out to meet her. The crews of the *Cambridge* and the other wooden vessels could do little but watch the historic slugfest unfold and root for the *Monitor,* which Cushing described as "something far from prepossessing in appearance and calculated to excite laughter. . . . The two ironclads now went to work in earnest, fighting at close quarters and exchanging iron blows that cracked sharp and distinct against adamantine sides and sent the echo miles off amongst us spectators, riveting us with intense interest to the scene."[22]

When the strange looking Union contestant managed to fight her formidable opponent to a standstill, the crews on the wooden ships felt an enormous sense of relief that soon gave way to unbridled rejoicing. Before the drama had ended, however, at 9:30 that morning, the *Cambridge* was ordered to Beaufort,

North Carolina. She immediately weighed anchor and stood down the bay.

Commander Parker received a report that the notorious Rebel paddle wheeler *Nashville* was in Beaufort. Before the war, the *Nashville* had been a passenger steamer that ran between Charleston and New York. After the fall of Fort Sumter, the Confederates had seized her in Charleston, slapped on a pair of 6-pounders, and used her as a cruiser. She had run into Beaufort on February 28, with a load of Enfield rifles from England after capturing two prizes worth $66,000. Shortly after her arrival, the Confederate government sold her to the private firm John Fraser and Company for use as a blockade-runner.

Cushing volunteered to lead a party into Beaufort to cut out the *Nashville,* which John Fraser and Company had renamed the *Thomas L. Wragg.* Commander Parker said no. Cushing seethed with anger at Parker's refusal, especially after the former *Nashville* slipped out of Beaufort and past the *Cambridge* on the night of March 17. Instead of "the blue and gold of a dashing service," Cushing hissed in his memoirs, Parker "should have worn petticoats."[23] Assistant Secretary of the Navy Gus Fox considered the *Nashville*'s escape as a "terrible blow to our prestige," as he put it in a letter to Flag Officer Louis M. Goldsborough, who had assumed command of the North Atlantic Blockading Squadron on September 23, 1861. "This is not blockade," Fox raged. "It is a Bull Run to the Navy."[24]

Shortly after the *Wragg* wriggled free of the blockade, Commander Parker sent Midshipman Cushing home on sick leave. A board of medical survey had declared him unfit for duty, for his hand had become badly infected and exposure while leading boarding parties over the winter had left him with a deep cough.

Cushing arrived home at the end of March. His mother put him to bed and, over the next several weeks, nursed him back to health. In May he received orders to return to the *Minnesota.* He reported for duty onboard before the month ended.

Meanwhile, Maj. Gen. George B. McClellan had launched his bid to end the war by marching more than 100,000 men up the peninsula between Virginia's York and James Rivers and capturing Richmond. The "Young Napoleon's" advance proved much slower than he had planned, but resulted in the recapture of Norfolk on May 10, 1862 and the destruction of the *Virginia* the next day, blown up by her crew to prevent her from falling into Union hands.

About a month after Cushing returned to the squadron, Confederate forces under Maj. Gen. Robert E. Lee, who had assumed command of the Army of Northern Virginia in early June, turned McClellan's stately advance into a speedy retreat in a series of battles lasting seven days, beginning on June 25. Although the Army of the Potomac outnumbered the Army of Northern Virginia and inflicted more casualties than it suffered during the Seven Days, McClellan was defeated. The Army of the Potomac retreated to Harrison's Landing on the James, where McClellan cowered under the protection of Navy gunboats.

Early in July Flag Officer Goldsborough called upon McClellan to discuss the general's request for naval support. Goldsborough brought Cushing along as a member of his staff. At that time, Abraham Lincoln also decided to call upon McClellan. The President's dissatisfaction with the general was growing daily, and he decided to inspect the Army of the Potomac himself. He arrived on July 7 and that evening rode along the lines reviewing the troops, who greeted him with hearty applause. Cushing rode with the President's entourage.

By this time, Will's brother Allie had been promoted to chief of ordnance on the staff of Brig. Gen. Edwin V. Sumner, one of McClellan's corps commanders. During the Seven Days, Allie displayed extraordinary courage under fire, delivering dispatches without regard for his own safety, having two horses shot out from under him, and taking a musket ball in the chest. Fortunately, the ball struck a dispatch book and a pistol he was carrying, and he escaped this brush with death uninjured.

Will couldn't resist the opportunity to visit his beloved brother, so he slipped away from Flag Officer Goldsborough without permission to spend time with Allie. Will sat spellbound as Allie regaled him with tales of his experiences during the Peninsula Campaign and determined to accompany his brother into the next fight. It quickly became apparent that McClellan had no intention of fighting again any time soon. Goldsborough, meanwhile, had returned to Norfolk.

After a brief absence of a few days, Will returned to Norfolk. Goldsborough was a more lenient squadron commander than Stringham had been. "I was placed under suspension for leaving my Admiral," Cushing later recalled. "But, as a midshipman is hardly considered a responsible being, was soon released."[25]

Instead of being punished, Cushing was promoted to lieutenant on July 16, jumping the grades of master and ensign. "I can glory in being the only man who has ever reached my rank at anywheres near my age," he wrote his mother. "Just think! A lieutenant in the most exclusive branch of the regular service. I rank with a captain in the regular army, and get nearly two thousand dollars a year, and I am not yet twenty." The pay, Will told his mother, was going to make life a lot easier. "I can, as regularly as clock work send home $50 monthly," he declared. "No more work for you, dear Mother. No more toil and sorrow for your children!"[26]

Cushing asked to serve under his old friend and mentor Charles W. Flusser, for Flusser, as Will told his mother, was "daring to the death," "chuck full of fight," and "the fighting man of the sounds."[27] Nearly five months after seizing the forts at Hatteras Inlet, Union naval and army forces launched an expedition into the sounds of eastern North Carolina, capturing Roanoke Island, Elizabeth City, New Bern, Morehead City, and Beaufort. By the summer of 1862, the entire North Carolina coast from the Virginia line to Cape Fear lay in Yankee hands. Wilmington on the Cape Fear River was the only North Carolina port remaining in Rebel hands. It soon became the Confederacy's premier port for blockade-runners. Flusser had been in the thick of it and was now a lieutenant commander and skipper of the side-wheel steamer *Commodore Perry,* a former New York City ferryboat that had been converted into a gunboat.

Cushing's request to serve under Flusser was granted, and he became the executive officer. Like the *Cambridge*, the *Commodore Perry* was perfectly suited for steaming along shallow waterways on missions deep inside enemy territory.

About two months after Cushing's arrival, the opportunity for just such a mission arose. On September 26, Maj. Gen. John A. Dix, who had relieved Ben Butler in command of the Department of Virginia, requested two or three gunboats to support an attack on the town of Franklin, Virginia. Franklin stood on the banks of the Blackwater River, a tributary of North Carolina's Chowan River, which empties into Albemarle Sound. General Dix had received reports that some 7,000 Confederate soldiers were massing near Franklin for an attack on the Union base at Suffolk, Virginia. He proposed to disperse this force and destroy the bridge across the Blackwater at Franklin. According to the plan, a sort of hammer-and-anvil operation, 12,000 troops under Dix would march west from Suffolk and drive the Rebels to the river, where the gunboats would block their escape across the bridge at Franklin. As senior naval officer in Albemarle Sound, Lieutenant Commander Flusser led the naval forces assigned to the mission.

Lack of communication between Army and Navy forces hampered the effectiveness of joint operations in the eastern theater throughout the Civil War, and the operation against Franklin was no exception. Flusser and Dix had agreed to launch the attack at 6 A.M. on October 3, but about five hours after the *Commodore Perry* and the gunboats *Hunchback* and *Whitehead* got underway, a courier arrived in Plymouth, North Carolina, with a message from Dix requesting Flusser to delay his departure for several days. Only 1,300 troops set out for Franklin, but they never got close to the bridge over the Blackwater. On October 2 the gunboats reached a point three miles below Franklin, where they anchored for the night. At 5:45 A.M. on the appointed morning, the *Commodore Perry, Hunchback,* and *Whitehead* headed upriver, shelling the banks as they went. The stream was narrow and crooked, and the sailors had to fasten lines to trees to heave the bows of the gunboats around the bends.

When the gunboats were rounding a bend about three-quarters of a mile below Franklin, Confederate soldiers concealed on a bluff overlooking the river opened fire. The soldiers were so close that the sailors couldn't elevate their guns enough to reach them, so Flusser ordered the men to take cover while the *Commodore Perry* steamed by. The gunboat grounded in the narrow channel, but managed to get unstuck and proceeded far enough upriver that she could bring her guns to bear on the soldiers. The *Commodore Perry* let loose with canister and grape, covering the *Hunchback* as she steamed by. The *Hunchback,* in turn, covered the *Whitehead.*

No sooner had the gunboats rounded the bend than they encountered a barricade across the river a quarter mile upstream and more Rebel soldiers on both banks. Unable to remove the barricade under the fire of the Rebel soldiers on the bluff and the banks, Flusser decided to hold the position and wait for Dix's men to arrive. Although reports of Rebel strength had been greatly exaggerated, they heavily outnumbered and outgunned the two hundred sailors and fourteen boat howitzers and heavy cannon on the steamers.

After more than three hours under Rebel fire, Flusser concluded that the Army wasn't coming. At 10:15 A.M., he decided to head back downriver. The Rebels tried to block their escape by felling trees across the river, but the gunboats got up a heavy head of steam and pushed through. Confederate soldiers kept the *Commodore Perry, Hunchback,* and *Whitehead* under fire for more than four hours while the gunboats struggled to get downstream, fighting to make every bend. Flusser admired Cushing for never flinching in the face of fire, but Flusser felt he was taking too many chances and told him time and again to duck. During the retreat, Cushing prevented a group of Rebel soldiers from boarding the *Commodore Perry* with a timely dose of canister from a boat gun. Although Cushing counted more than a thousand bullet marks on the *Commodore Perry,* losses among the crews of all three gunboats totaled only four killed and fifteen wounded.

Cushing received a good deal of recognition for his exploits during the battle. Flusser, in his report to Comdr. Henry K. Davenport, the senior naval officer in the North Carolina sounds, declared the young officer "worthy of praise for great gallantry." Acting Rear Adm. Samuel Phillips Lee, who had relieved Flag Officer Goldsborough as commander of the North Atlantic Blockading Squadron on September 4, reported to Gideon Welles that Cushing was "increasing his reputation by active operations."[28] In a letter to Cousin Mary, Cushing bragged about being "the only officer mentioned in Capt. Flusser's official report for special gallantry in action" in what he declared to be "one of the hardest fights that the Navy has had during the war."[29]

Cushing received more than praise for his role in the battle. He also got command of the gunboat *Ellis,* a small iron side-wheeler tug armed with two guns captured from the Confederates at Elizabeth City. Cushing didn't let the *Ellis's* modest size affect his own modesty, however. "I can justly be proud of having command of a steamer at the age of nineteen," he wrote Cousin Mary. "It is a thing unheard of in the service."[30]

During the rest of October, the *Ellis* operated in the vicinity of Beaufort. Cushing's mission was to intercept any Rebel trade running through Bogue Inlet. The duty was pleasant enough. Every day Cushing sent a party ashore to kill a cow, hog, or sheep to provide fresh meat for the twenty-eight-man crew.

But Cushing wanted more action. After two days with nothing happening at Bogue Inlet, Cushing left his assigned station and steamed southward to New Topsail Inlet, where he had heard that blockade-runners were also operating. After steaming through New Topsail Inlet at full speed, Cushing spotted a vessel about a mile in. The crew of the vessel fled at the *Ellis's* approach. Cushing sent over a boarding party. The prize proved to be the schooner *Adelaide,* ready to sail to Bermuda with a cargo of six hundred barrels of turpentine, thirty-six bales of cotton, and some tobacco. Cushing took the prize in tow, but the schooner drew too much water and kept grounding, so he torched the vessel.

Although Cushing had "somewhat exceeded the letter of his instructions by leaving his station," as Commander Davenport put it in a report to Admiral Lee, Davenport approved of his action. He ordered Cushing to "continue to act in accordance with the dictates of your best judgement and discretion." This gave Cushing a "roving commission," as he put it in a letter to Cousin Mary, to intercept enemy trade and conduct raids ashore.[31]

Cushing wasted no time in finding more action. On October 29, he returned to New Topsail Inlet. About three-quarters of a mile in, he discovered a large saltworks ashore, big enough to "have furnished all Wilmington with salt," as he put it in his official report.[32] Salt was a scarce and valuable commodity in the Confederacy. Cushing led a party ashore, tore down the brickwork, destroyed the large copper kettles and iron pans, cut holes in the lighters and flatboats, stove in the cisterns, and burned the buildings. Just as the Yankees were getting ready to leave, some Rebel soldiers opened fire on them with muskets and two pieces of artillery. Cushing got back on board the *Ellis* and returned fire, scattering the Rebels. Cushing's crew suffered no casualties.

On November 23, Cushing launched a raid on the town of Jacksonville, North Carolina, the seat of Onslow County, some thirty-five or forty miles up the New River. Cushing intended to capture any vessels he saw on the river, destroy any saltworks he found along its banks, land at Onslow court house, and capture the Wilmington mail, from which he hoped to glean valuable information. Five miles up from New River Inlet, the *Ellis* encountered an outbound vessel loaded with cotton and turpentine. The vessel's crew set her on fire to prevent her from falling into Union hands. Cushing reached Onslow court house at 1 P.M. and sent a landing party ashore. The Yankees captured the mail as planned, along with twenty-five stands of arms, two schooners, and the Confederate postmaster's slaves. The *Ellis* got back underway at 2:30 P.M. with the schooners in tow. As the tug headed downriver, Cushing shelled a Rebel encampment at one point and engaged some infantry near the schooner he had encountered on the way up, which was still burning.

With both daylight and the tide on the wane, Cushing decided to spend the night a few miles upriver from the outer bar and make a dash for the inlet in the morning. All night long the crew could see enemy signal fires along the banks of the river. Cushing got the *Ellis* underway at first light and soon came under fire from two Confederate cannons on the south bank. The sailors returned fire and drove the Rebels away from their guns, but the pair of pilots on board the *Ellis* misread the channel and the tug ran hard aground. The sailors spent the rest of the day trying to free the *Ellis,* but their efforts were in vain.

Cushing figured that the Rebels would return in force the next day. When darkness fell, he had everything except his heavier cannon loaded onto one of the prizes, then ordered his sailors on board. He called for six volunteers to remain and fight with him on the *Ellis.* He ordered the schooner to drop down the channel out of range of the bluffs and wait. If the Rebels destroyed the tug, the schooner was to head to sea. Evidently, he ordered the other prize schooner destroyed.

At daylight the Rebels opened a heavy crossfire on the *Ellis* with four artillery pieces. The seven Yankees on the tug fought back as best they could, but it soon became clear to Cushing that "the only alternatives left," as he put it in his report to Commander Davenport, "were surrender or a pull of one and a half miles under their fire in my small boat. The first of these was not, of course, to be thought of; the second I resolved to attempt."[33]

Cushing torched the *Ellis,* then he and the others boarded the boat, rowed to the schooner, and set sail for the sea. "It was low water on the bar and a heavy surf was rolling in," Cushing noted, "but the wind forced us through after striking several times."[34] The schooner got away in the nick of time, just as several companies of cavalry were galloping toward the mouth of the inlet to cut off the Yankees' escape. The men gave three cheers, and the schooner reached Beaufort four hours later. Somehow the crew escaped injury, but they left behind the Wilmington mail. Cushing submitted a brief report from memory on the contents of the mailbag, but it was no substitute for the real thing.

Cushing ended his official report of the raid with a request for a court of inquiry "to investigate the facts of the case, and to see if the honor of the flag has suffered in my hands." But far from condemning Cushing, both Commander Davenport and Admiral Lee commended him for his "coolness, courage, and conduct."[35] Cushing received a few days leave, which he spent resting in New Bern and visiting friends and family in Fredonia.

Meanwhile, the Navy and War Departments were planning a joint operation against Wilmington, North Carolina. Like the plan for the attack on Franklin, troops and warships were to proceed to the objective independently. Army forces were to march inland from New Bern, sever the Wilmington and Weldon Railroad, over which the Rebels ran arms and ammunition through the blockade to the Army of Northern Virginia, then turn on Wilmington from the north. Indeed, the plan was already unfolding, for some 11,000 Union soldiers had set out from New Bern on December 11 and in less than a week had won battles at Kinston, Whitehall, and Goldsboro, reaching the railroad at the last town.

The Navy was to push a flotilla of gunboats up the Cape Fear River and approach Wilmington from the south. Among the stumbling blocks in the Navy's plan was the lack of pilots for navigating the Cape Fear River's intricate bars. When Cushing returned to duty that December, he put forth a scheme to remedy the problem by capturing some pilots. He proposed to disguise his prize schooner as an English blockade-runner, have a blockader pretend to chase her under the guns of Fort Caswell, the principal Confederate work guarding Old Inlet, the southern entrance to the Cape Fear River, take a pilot on board as though the schooner was going on to Wilmington, then turn around and head straight for the sea, "trusting to the boldness of the affair to carry me clear," as he put it in his memoirs.[36]

Commander Davenport had Cushing run the plan past Admiral Lee. "Young Cushing's scheme ventures more than it promises," Lee wrote Assistant Secretary Fox on December 11, "but liking the morale of the thing I would not stop the project."[37] Fox thought that "rashness in a young officer is rather commendable."[38] Cushing received the go-ahead on the day after Christmas 1862.

Unfortunately, the winds off Cape Fear weren't blowing hard enough, and the Rebels spotted the becalmed vessel loitering among the blockaders well before he had a chance to get started. Cushing didn't abandon the idea of plucking pilots and improvised another plan to capture a pilot or two along with schooners reported to be at a pilot station on Little River, South Carolina, some thirty miles below Fort Caswell.

Cushing's schooner reached Little River Inlet on the morning of January 5, 1863. At 8:00 P.M. under the cover of darkness, he led a party of twenty-five men in three cutters over the bar and upriver. They had gone about a mile when Confederate soldiers on a bluff spotted them and opened fire. Cushing beached the boats about two hundred yards from the bluff, formed up the men, and gave the orders "forward; double quick; charge."[39]

When the sailors got clear of the woods, Cushing saw a fort by the flickering light of Confederate campfires. He figured that the Rebels had no idea how many men he had, so he ordered his men to charge the works with fixed bayonets. His idea had the intended effect, for as his men scrambled over one side of the earthworks "yelling like demons," the startled defenders skedaddled over the other.[40] The Rebels departed so hastily that they had left behind their stores, clothing, ammunition, many of their arms, and a supper of pork and greens. Cushing concluded that they had run off a company of infantry that greatly outnumbered his force, so he decided not to linger long. He and his men had a quick bite to eat, took what they could, destroyed what they couldn't, and searched the area for pilots. They soon got into another skirmish and, after firing all their ammunition, got back in the boats and returned to the schooner. They suffered only one casualty, a man shot in the leg. Although Cushing neither captured any pilots nor saw any of the Rebel schooners reported to be there, Admiral Lee forwarded Cushing's report of the mission to Secretary Welles with an endorsement stating that the feat "does great credit to the gallantry of this promising young officer."[41]

To reward Cushing for his initiative and to inspire more such initiative, Admiral Lee intended to give Cushing a new ship. But first, Cushing was given twelve more days of leave, which he spent in Washington. "Mud and contractors were thick in the streets," he wrote Cousin Mary, "and it was impossible to keep from soiling my hands clothes &c by contact with one or the other." He stayed with his oldest brother, Milton, who was rooming in a boarding house. Milt had joined the Navy in 1861 and was working in the Navy Department. During Will's visit, the two brothers took in a number of comedies at the city's theaters. They didn't see as many tragedies, because Milt would invariably crack up laughing at an actor's line at an inappropriate moment, "much to the amazement and sometimes indignation of the surrounding multitude," as Will put it.[42]

Toward the end of Cushing's leave, Gideon Welles summoned him to the Navy Department and offered him command of one of two ships: the *Violet,* a fast steamer slated to chase blockade-runners off Wilmington, or the larger, slower *Commodore Barney.* A converted New York ferryboat like the *Commodore Perry,* the 512-ton *Commodore Barney* was a significantly larger vessel than the 100-ton *Ellis,* armed with seven guns and crewed by 150 men, but she was still small enough to operate in shallow waters deep behind enemy lines. Cushing chose the *Commodore Barney.* "The command of her belongs to some officer of a higher grade than myself," he wrote Cousin Mary, "but they (the powers that be) are pleased to think that I have earned the distinction. Of course I am as proud as a peacock at being the only Lieut. in the regular Navy who has a command."[43]

During the late winter and early spring of 1863, the *Commodore Barney* operated in the vicinity of Hampton Roads on blockade duty. Cushing found the duty dull at times, but as he wrote to Cousin Mary on April 5, "a brisk correspondence helps to do away with the spare time." Will hadn't heard much from Mary lately, however. "The last time that I had a letter from you was in December," he lamented. "I only look at one thing and that is the gradual falling off of the old correspondence that we kept up so long."[44] No doubt Cousin Mary's baby girl, who had been born in the fall of 1862, occupied much of the time she used to have for writing to Will.

On several occasions Cushing had the opportunity to dine with Admiral Lee. The young lieutenant spun yarns about how Henry Davenport dealt with the sutlers and traders in the North Carolina sounds, and the old admiral laughed heartily. Every now and then Cushing dropped hints to the admiral that he wanted to be sent back down to the sounds, "but up to this time he has not been made to see the propriety of it," as Cushing put it in a letter to Henry Davenport.[45]

Will wasn't long in command of the *Commodore Barney* before the war spiced up his life again. On April 11, Rebel forces under Lt. Gen. James Longstreet advanced on Suffolk, Virginia, as part of a coordinated Confederate offensive launched that spring in eastern North Carolina and southeastern Virginia. Suffolk stood on the Nansemond River about fifteen miles southwest of Norfolk. Advancing from the west and south, Longstreet intended to pin or capture Union forces in Suffolk, enabling him to fill his supply wagons with tons of bacon and salted fish east of the Blackwater and Chowan Rivers without interference.

Maj. Gen. John J. Peck, commander of the Union forces in the region, found himself outnumbered two to one. He feared that if Confederate forces crossed the Nansemond River above Suffolk, got behind him, and cut his line of communications, all would be lost. On April 11, Maj. Gen. E. D. Keyes, in command of the Army of the Potomac's Fourth Army Corps and Peck's immediate superior, asked Admiral Lee to send gunboats up the Nansemond. Early the next morning, Lee received an urgent message that the Rebels were, in fact, attempting to cross the Nansemond in an effort to surround Suffolk.

To prevent Confederate forces from crossing the river, Admiral Lee sent the river steamer *Mount Washington*, the tugs *Alert* and *Cohasset*, and the converted ferryboat *Stepping Stones* to op-

erate in the upper Nansemond between Suffolk and the junction
with the Western Branch. "The upper Nansemond is seven miles
long and difficult to navigate," Lee informed Gideon Welles, "as
it is very crooked and narrow and has some bad bars. It is, in
fact, a mere creek."[46] Lt. Roswell Hanks Lamson, skipper of the
Mount Washington, commanded the flotilla.

Admiral Lee sent the *Commodore Barney* to cover the lower
Nansemond, a much broader and straighter stretch of the river
between the Western Branch and Hampton Roads. "When
there," Lee ordered Cushing, "act at your discretion." Since
Cushing was senior to Lamson, he had overall command.[47]

On April 12, Cushing communicated with both General Peck
and Lieutenant Lamson. For Cushing and Lamson, the meeting
marked the beginning of a beautiful friendship. Lamson had
been a year behind Cushing at the Naval Academy and, like
Cushing, was earning a reputation as one of the Union Navy's
boldest and most skilful young officers.

The gunboats traded fire with Confederate batteries all that
day and the next. On April 14 the *Mount Washington, Stepping
Stones,* and Army steamer *West End* were steaming downstream
from Suffolk and discovered newly erected Rebel earthworks
thrown up at a sharp bend in the river a few miles below the
town. The gunboats shelled the earthworks briefly, then Lamson
signaled for them to run by. At that moment, the Confederates
unmasked seven artillery pieces and opened fire, putting a shot
through the *Mount Washington*'s boilers and causing the *West
End* to run aground. The *Stepping Stones* towed the disabled vessels all the way down toward the obstructions at the mouth of
the Western Branch under fire from Rebel sharpshooters the
whole way. The tide was low, and when the *Mount Washington*
reached the bar at the mouth of the Western Branch, she ran
aground. At that moment, the Rebels opened a murderous crossfire on the vessels from ten guns on Hill's Point, where the Western Branch flowed into the Nansemond.

Cushing moved toward the sound of the guns and positioned
the *Commodore Barney* as close to the disabled *Mount Washing-*

ton as his deeper draft would permit. For the next five hours Lamson and Cushing fought Confederate gunners and sharp-shooters ashore, twice driving the Rebels away from their positions. As the tide came up, the *Mount Washington* floated free and her crew moved her out of range by sending lines ashore to warp her down the river. Losses from all the vessels engaged totaled five dead, fourteen wounded, and one missing, believed dead, with ten of the casualties from the *Commodore Barney.* The *Mount Washington* was pretty well shot up, "completely riddled in hull and machinery," as Lamson put it.[48]

Lamson credited Cushing with saving his ship. Cushing "supported me throughout the action in the most gallant manner," Lamson wrote in his official report to Lee. "It was owing in a great measure to his well-directed fire, causing the enemy to shift his position, that the Mount Washington was not entirely destroyed."[49]

Cushing maintained his station on the lower Nansemond for the next several days, shelling Rebel positions ashore and frequently coming under musket or artillery fire from Hill's Point, which had become the most dangerous point on the river for the Navy, as vessels attempting to pass by came within fifty yards of the Rebel battery there. Cushing noticed civilians working closely with the Confederate soldiers. "The people living in this vicinity aid the Rebels in every way," Cushing reported to Lee. "If I take one with arms in his hands trying to kill my men, I will not take him prisoner."[50] Cushing posted pickets on the west bank every night to prevent Rebel forces from launching a surprise attack on his vessel from the wooded bank.

On April 18, Admiral Lee ordered Lamson to withdraw from the upper Nansemond. Army forces, Lee declared, were better suited to defend the narrow part of the river from positions on the east bank. He told Cushing to keep patrolling the lower Nansemond to prevent the Rebels from erecting defenses on the west bank.

Three days later, Acting Master T. A. Harris spotted a civilian on the bank waving a white handkerchief. He sent five sailors ashore in a boat to see what the man wanted. As soon as the boat landed, Confederate soldiers hidden in the brush ambushed the sailors, killing one and capturing the others.

The ambush infuriated Cushing, who organized a raid in retaliation. Seeking to recapture the sailors and to make the Rebels think twice about doing such a thing again, he mustered seven boats, seventy-five sailors from the vessels under his command, and fifteen soldiers from the Army vessel *West End*. Early the next afternoon, he landed the men and a boat gun at the point where the trap had been sprung. He secured the body of the sailor killed in the ambush, burned all the houses in the vicinity, then led his men inland to Chuckatuck, a village located on Chuckatuck Creek, three miles from the Nansemond behind enemy lines. Cushing believed the Rebels had taken his sailors to the village. Intelligence indicated that four hundred Confederate cavalry were posted there.

About a mile and a half from the village, the sailors drove in the enemy pickets and captured a mule-drawn cart to which they limbered the boat gun. At 4:30 P.M. they entered the streets of the village. Suddenly, forty cavalry appeared around a corner two hundred yards in front of them, drew their sabers, and charged. Cushing unlimbered the boat gun and his men opened fire, killing two of the cavalrymen and scaring the captured mules, who bolted toward the oncoming horsemen, taking the cart and most of the ammunition for the boat gun with them. Cushing ordered the gun crew to reload with canister. "All gone in the mule cart, sir!" replied one of the men.[51] Cushing then ordered his men forward. With a cheer the sailors charged the cavalry! The astonished horsemen scattered, leaving Cushing in possession of the village. The Yankees lost one man dead in the skirmish. When Cushing learned that the Rebels had taken the captured sailors somewhere else, he marched the men back to the boats, engaging in a small skirmish along the way. He reached the Nansemond safely at 7:00 P.M. and had the bodies of the sailors killed in the ambush and in Chuckatuck taken to one of the gunboats. Cushing concluded from his "reconnaissance," as he reported to Admiral Lee, that the Rebels were "not in strong force near Suffolk." In a dispatch to Secretary Welles, Admiral Lee praised Cushing's "zeal, courage, and discretion."[52]

The Navy Department sent Cushing a letter of commendation for the raid on Chuckatuck. "Your gallantry and meritorious services," Gideon Welles said in the letter, "are entitled to the especial notice . . . of the Department. Your conduct on this occasion adds additional luster to the character you had already established for valor in the face of the enemy."[53] The official recognition symbolized Cushing's arrival at a position of prominence in the naval officer corps. The young lieutenant had had a rough ride supplanting the reputation as a troublemaker he had earned at the academy with the reputation for steely courage in the face of the enemy he had earned on the Nansemond. But from now on, the question was not whether to keep him in the Navy, but how best to use him.

For the next three weeks, Cushing remained on the Nansemond, trading shots with Rebel sharpshooters and flying batteries and making occasional forays ashore as combat along the Nansemond wound down. Longstreet withdrew from the area on the night of May 4 to join with Robert E. Lee's Army of Northern Virginia against the Army of the Potomac, which had crossed the Rappahannock River on April 27. Longstreet's men got moving too late, however, to take part in General Lee's greatest victory, the battle of Chancellorsville, which had reached a climax the day before. On May 5, General Peck reported to his superiors that the siege of Suffolk and Longstreet's thrust into southeastern Virginia and the sounds of North Carolina had ended, and he praised the conduct of Cushing, Lamson, and their men.

Being the target of Rebel artillery and small-arms fire nearly every day for almost a month left the *Commodore Barney* so badly shot up that Cushing was ordered to take her to Baltimore for repairs. It took shipyard workers six weeks to put the old ferryboat right again, giving Cushing a respite from combat.

Cushing spent three of those weeks in Boston. His mother was there, as were many of his friends and acquaintances. "I must say that I never have enjoyed myself before as I did there," he wrote Cousin Mary. "I had a dozen different engagements a day; laughed, talked, smoked, enjoyed the society of ladies, had some grand rides, good fishing, and some splendid dinners on the sea beach."[54]

A few lines down, the same letter revealed that two years of Civil War had not blunted Cushing's racism, but had sharpened it. "The only thing that disgusted me [in Boston]," he wrote, "was the freedom with which abolitionists can talk. And then to see a black greasy darkey, coolly retaining his seat in a horse car while ladies are standing. I heard of this, but did not, thank fortune, get my eye on one of the scoundrels, or there would have been a naval officer tried for killing a 'free and equal, though unfortunately black American citizen.'" Although Cushing couched his diatribe in terms of gentlemanly conduct toward ladies, it was prejudice of this sort that kept African Americans in a state of near bondage for another century after the Civil War.[55]

Cushing spent the other three weeks in Washington, going to the theater with his brother Milt and commuting by train to Baltimore to monitor the progress of repairs on the *Commodore Barney*. The highlight of Cushing's spring break was a meeting with Abraham Lincoln arranged by Gideon Welles. Cushing realized that his star had risen. "I am in high favor with the [Navy] Department now," he wrote Cousin Mary, "and can do about as I please."[56]

Chapter 4

Darkest Moment, Brightest Moment

USHING RETURNED to active duty in June 1863, once again in command of the *Commodore Barney*. On June 29, he received orders to take his ship to Washington. Robert E. Lee was moving north, launching an offensive into Pennsylvania. Lee wanted "to fight a climactic battle on Northern soil," as historian Emory Thomas puts it, seeking "a showdown, a battle of annihilation that would end the war in a single afternoon."[1] The Navy Department wanted Cushing's gunboat available to help defend the capital, if it came to that.

Robert E. Lee did, in fact, lead the Army of Northern Virginia into the greatest battle of the Civil War on July 1–3 at Gettysburg. Alonzo Cushing performed brilliantly during the first two days. "He is," remarked Maj. Gen. Winfield Scott Hancock, who had witnessed his exploits on July 2, "the bravest man I ever saw."[2] On the third day, fate placed the six guns of Allie's Battery A, Fourth U.S. Artillery, on Cemetery Ridge, just north of the copse of trees where the battle reached its climax.

At about 1:00 P.M., Confederate artillery on Seminary Ridge opened a furious cannonade that seemed to concentrate on the copse of trees. The bombardment knocked out three of Cushing's guns and killed and wounded most of his men. A shell fragment ripped open Allie's thighs and genitals. Though in agonizing pain, he refused to give up command.

After some time passed—some said half an hour, others said two hours—the bombardment lifted, the smoke cleared, and fifteen thousand Southerners moved out for an assault known forever after as Pickett's Charge. Lee had designated the copse of trees as their goal. Allie fired round after round of double canister at the onrushing gray tide. Confederate soldiers fired back. One bullet struck Allie in the shoulder, another hit him in the stomach, and still, he stood by his gun. While he was shouting orders a third bullet entered his open mouth, finally killing him. The Confederate tide swept over him, reaching its high watermark a few yards past where he lay. There, the Confederate assault foundered under a withering Union fire from three sides.

Will learned of his favorite brother's death hours later and set out for Gettysburg that evening. Will sought to secure Allie's body and lead Battery A in the next battle. "The field, when I reached it, was a sickening sight," Will wrote in his memoirs.

> Thirty thousand wounded men and thousands of unburied dead lay on the earth, in road, field, wood and orchard, and under the scorching sun on the bare hillside amidst all the wreck of a great battle. Dismounted cannon, dead horses, exploded caissons and broken muskets were everywhere and the artillery position on Cemetery [Ridge] was almost paved with the Rebel iron that had been hurled by the hundred and fifty guns massed against it previous to the final charge. My brother's battery was destroyed. Five out of the six guns were dismounted, all the officers and most of the men were shot and seventy of its horses stiffened upon the wooded knoll where they were placed for shelter.[3]

Will Cushing achieved neither of his aims at Gettysburg: there was nothing left of his brother's battery for him to command, and his brother's remains were already on a train bound for West Point, where they would be laid to rest. As there was nothing really for him to do, Will returned to Washington, devastated by Allie's death.

For Will it was the war's darkest moment. He remained in the capital for the next several weeks with his brother Milt, struggling to cope with the loss. It is not known how many tears he shed or how many fantasies of revenge he indulged in.

At the end of July, the Navy Department relieved him of command of the *Commodore Barney* and placed him in command of the *Shokokon,* yet another converted ferryboat. By then he had dealt with his grief at Allie's loss well enough to attempt some humor and to try to comfort his mother. On July 30, he wrote her about the new ship and its "jaw-breaking indian name." He told her that he was going to Wilmington to hunt "anglo-rebel steamers," as he and many of his peers called blockade-runners. "Look out for prize money." "I long to hear from you, dear Mother, and to know that you do not feel utterly lonely and sad," he added. "Think how many children you have left, and how dearly they love you."[4]

Cushing arrived off Wilmington in August 1863, and it wasn't long before he got back in action. On August 20, Cushing asked permission to cut out a schooner he had discovered earlier at a wharf on Virginia Creek some six miles up from New Topsail Inlet. Capt. Benjamin F. Sands, the officer in command of the blockaders off of Old Inlet, denied Cushing's request, arguing that he didn't want to take responsibility for the "risk of life," as Cushing put it in his memoir.[5] Chafed by Sands's refusal, Cushing decided to conduct the mission anyway.

On August 22, Cushing sent two boatloads of sailors ashore on the beach several miles above the schooner. Six sailors and an officer carried a dinghy through the brush across the barrier island that separated the sea from the sound and approached the schooner from the north. Meanwhile, the *Shokokon* made a demonstration at sea close to the beach below the schooner, drawing the Rebels' attention to the south. The seven men in the dinghy sneaked up on the schooner from behind, surprised the guards, and captured ten soldiers, eighteen horses, and a 12-pounder howitzer. With the help of slaves from nearby plantations, the sailors burned the schooner and a nearby saltworks. The sailors brought three of the prisoners back to the *Shokokon* in the dinghy, but left the slaves to their fate. The sailors accomplished the mission without loss to themselves. "I never was credited officially with this," Cushing noted in his memoirs, "perhaps because I disobeyed orders, or, maybe, for the reason that the great fish present could not surrender so dainty a morsel to a youngster."[6]

On August 27 the *Shokokon* got caught in a gale off New Inlet, the northern entrance to the Cape Fear River. Cushing quickly discovered that the former New York ferryboat wasn't built for weathering gales in the ocean, for the heavy seas opened her seams, causing her to leak at the rate of 450 gallons of water per minute. "When struck by a sea forward," Cushing reported to Admiral Lee, "she seemed to give and bend like india rubber."[7] Cushing declared her unfit for blockade duty.

Admiral Lee concurred, sent the *Shokokon* to Hampton Roads for repairs, and gave Cushing dispatches to deliver to the Navy Department. One of Lee's dispatches did, in fact, involve the burning of the schooner. Instead of reprimanding Cushing for disobeying orders, however, Admiral Lee praised the mission and took credit for approving it in advance.

When Cushing arrived in Washington, Assistant Secretary Fox made him skipper of the gunboat *Monticello,* then undergoing repairs in Philadelphia. "You are ordered to this command," Fox told Cushing, "for distinguished services rendered."[8] The *Monticello* was larger, faster, and more seaworthy than any vessel Cushing had yet commanded. In fact, she was one of the fastest ships in the North Atlantic Blockading Squadron. Cushing spent the next several months getting her fitted out. He handpicked as many of the crew as he could. One young officer, Acting Master's Mate William. L. Howorth, particularly impressed him. In September Cushing managed to slip away for a weeklong visit to Fredonia. His mother seemed very old and was still immersed in grief for Allie. In November, he spent a night in jail in Philadelphia for "thrashing" a few "copperheads"—Democrats opposed to the war—who insulted him during the electioneering, as he recalled, "because I wore the uniform of my country's navy."[9]

Cushing returned to blockade duty off Wilmington in February 1864. By day the blockaders anchored out of range of the Rebel artillery ashore. By night ships patrolled close in to shore, their lead-gray hulls enabling them to blend in with fog and foam. Cushing stayed awake all night, getting his sleep in the afternoons.

It wasn't long before the routine of blockade duty bored him. To liven things up a bit, he decided to celebrate Washington's birthday by leading a cutting-out expedition past Fort Caswell and into the harbor near Smithville, a little town near the inlet and about twenty-four miles by water down from Wilmington. On the night of February 22, Cushing led forty men in three boats into the harbor as planned, but there were no vessels at the anchorage, so he turned back.

So that he wouldn't return empty handed on the way out, he thought he would dash ashore onto Smith's Island and snatch the flag from the Rebel battery at the point of land forming the eastern boundary of the inlet. As his gig drew near the battery, one of the oars banged on the wall of the fortification. Cushing figured he'd had it, but nobody in the battery reacted to the noise. With the guard so lax, Cushing perceived a golden opportunity to return with a bigger force and capture the battery and occupy the entire island, thereby closing off one of the entrances to the Cape Fear River. He returned to the fleet, reported to Captain Sands, and laid out his proposal. "Can't take the responsibility," replied Sands.[10]

This was the second time Sands refused to allow Cushing to conduct one of his special operations, and it angered him. He vowed to bring the local Confederate general to breakfast, then stormed off. Brig. Gen. Louis Hébert, Confederate commander of Fort Caswell, had his headquarters in Smithville. "My plan

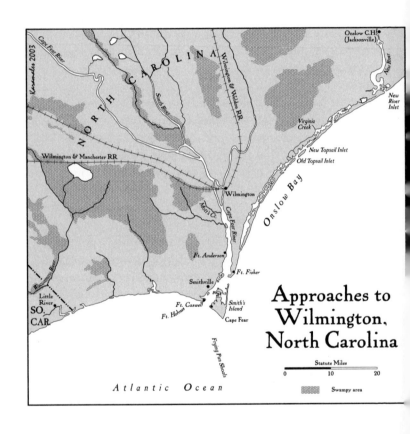

Approaches to Wilmington, North Carolina

was too bold to fail," Cushing wrote in his memoirs. "My object was to take the commanding general from his bed, in the midst of his men, and to take him out of the harbor in one of his own steamers."[11]

At 8:40 P.M. on the night of February 29, 1864, Cushing embarked on the mission, leading twenty men in two boats. With oars muffled, they crossed the bar and passed Fort Caswell without being seen and, after about a two-mile pull, landed at Smithville's waterfront. While the men hid the boats under a wharf and concealed themselves against the bank, Cushing captured two slaves from a nearby saltworks. The slaves told him where the Confederate soldiers were quartered and where sentries were posted in and around Smithville. Cushing returned to his men, then he, Howorth, Acting Ens. John E. Jones, and a sailor set out for General Hébert's residence, using one of the slaves as a guide.

The group crept down the street until they reached Hébert's residence, a large house with a big veranda. Across the street stood a barracks housing perhaps a hundred or more Rebel soldiers. Cushing motioned for his three men to "surround" Hébert's residence. He then eased over to the front door, opened it, and slipped inside. He crept past the dining room and up the stairs. At the top of the stairs, he lit a match, then opened one of the bedroom doors. Suddenly, he heard a crash downstairs. Cushing ran downstairs, pushed open the door to the room where the sound seemed to have come from, and struck another match. The flare of the match revealed a man standing inside, holding a chair, ready to strike. Cushing rushed him and knocked him down. With one hand on the man's throat and the other pointing a revolver at his temple, Cushing threatened to kill him if he spoke. The man nodded. Cushing got up, lit a candle, and asked the prisoner a few questions. The fellow turned out to be Capt. Patrick Kelly, General Hébert's chief engineer. Kelly said that the general was in Wilmington on business.

Suddenly Howorth rushed into the room and shouted that he had seen someone running away from the house toward the woods. It was W. D. Hardeman, the Confederate adjutant general. Hardeman had been asleep in another room downstairs, but Cushing's creeping about had awoken him. He looked out his open window, saw Howorth's big Navy revolver, and slammed the window shut, making the crashing noise that Cushing had heard. While Cushing was wrestling with Kelly, Hardeman slipped out the back door and bolted for the woods nearby.

Cushing snatched up some papers, barely gave Kelly time to pull on a pair of pants, and hustled him out the door and down the street. They reached the boats without being seen. No ships were in the harbor, so Cushing had to return in the boats. He and his men shoved off, taking Kelly and the slaves from the saltworks with them. It wasn't until the boats got near Fort Caswell that Confederate signal lights indicated that Yankee boats were in the harbor, and the alarm was sounded.

The raiding party returned to the *Monticello* by about 1:00 A.M. Cushing took Kelly to his cabin, gave him dry socks and a glass of sherry, and had a few laughs at his expense. The papers Cushing had snatched turned out to be worthless.

The next morning, Cushing brought Kelly to breakfast, astonishing Captain Sands. That afternoon, Cushing sent Acting Ensign Jones ashore under a flag of truce to pick up some clothing for Kelly. A Confederate colonel met the boat and escorted Jones to the telegraph office. The men had walked some distance in silence when the Confederate colonel suddenly wheeled around. "That was a damned splendid affair, sir!" he exclaimed. Jones and the colonel chatted amicably and were soon joined by the fellow who had barely escaped the night before. The Confederates gave Jones clothing for Kelly. Jones handed the colonel a note from Cushing, addressed to Hébert. "My Dear General," it said. "I deeply regret that you were not at home when I called. I enclose my card. Very respectfully, W. B. Cushing."[12]

Gideon Welles was so impressed with the news of Cushing's mission that he sent the young officer a letter complimenting him on his "gallantry." Welles liked Cushing's special operations.[13]

So did Sam Lee. Somehow Admiral Lee had caught wind of Cushing's proposal to capture Smith's Island. Although Lee thought the idea a long shot at best, he admired the young officer's "éclat" and "dash." "I like enterprises," he told Gus Fox, "and have always encouraged them." "I have a good idea of," he added, "and good feeling for this youngster."[14]

Gus Fox liked Cushing's special operations too, but wished they were more productive. "What a pity that Cushing's undaunted courage and good luck cannot be put to a useful purpose in a manner to tell upon the enemy," he wrote Sam Lee. What a pity that "so much luck and dash had not brought fruits equal to the risk." However, Fox wanted Cushing to keep trying. "You know the Department never finds fault with these exploits," he added. "I believe they ought to be encouraged. To be sure, the people will say, when he is captured, 'Damned fool.'" But Fox didn't feel that way. "You may be very sure that the Department will not find any fault with any dashing expeditions that give reasonable hope of a result injurious to the enemy," he said, "even though they fail occasionally."[15]

In early April Cushing proposed a new "enterprise"; he asked Admiral Lee to give him a "roving commission" to hunt for prizes independent of the blockade lines. Lee granted his request. Cushing didn't have much luck at it. All he managed to achieve the first month was to chase one ship, which got away, and to pick up an abandoned schooner loaded with rotten bananas and coconuts.

The Rebels soon gave Cushing another idea for the kind of operation more to his liking. On the night of May 6, 1864, the Confederate ironclad *Raleigh* emerged from the Cape Fear River and attacked the blockaders off New Inlet. Over the course of some four to six hours she traded shots with a total of five Union ships and managed to drive the smaller blockaders away from the bar for a few hours. None of the vessels on either side sustained significant damage. On the way back into the Cape Fear River on May 7, the *Raleigh* ran aground and broke her back. It was typical of the bad luck that the Rebels had with most of their ironclads.

Nobody on the Union side knew that the *Raleigh* had rendered herself hors de combat, however. As soon as Cushing heard of the "mortifying affair off Wilmington," as he described the fleeing of the wooden vessels, he felt obligated to eliminate the ironclad threat. "I deem it my duty to leave for the point of danger at once," he wrote Admiral Lee. He declared his intention to ram the *Raleigh* if she reappeared, promising to "go over her or to the bottom."[16]

Nearly two weeks passed without the *Raleigh* reappearing. If she wasn't going to come out, Cushing figured he'd have to go in and get her. He devised a plan for a night operation to lead a handpicked crew of men in small boats past the forts to the ironclad's reported anchorage at Smithville, board her, and either bring her out himself or sink her. He submitted the plan to both Captain Sands and Admiral Lee for approval. As usual, Sands didn't want to take responsibility for authorizing such a mission and turned Cushing down. When Lee didn't reply fast enough to suit him, Cushing went over his head, straight to the top, and proposed the operation to the secretary of the Navy.

Gideon Welles, of course, heartily approved the mission. "Risks to accomplish an important object ought to be undertaken without hesitation," he wrote Lee, "and will never be disapproved by the Department if well arranged and intrusted to good officers."[17] Welles directed Lee to order Sands to comply with Cushing's request for men and boats. Sands, of course, was not happy about Cushing's impertinence in going over his head, but at least now he wouldn't have to take the blame if the mission failed. Cushing, of course, was not happy about Sands's holding up the mission. "It was disgraceful to delay it an hour!" he later wrote.[18]

Cushing figured he'd better make a thorough reconnaissance before actually attempting to board the *Raleigh*. At 8 P.M. on June 23, Cushing, William Howorth, John Jones, and fifteen enlisted volunteers armed with cutlasses and small arms set out from the *Monticello* in a cutter and headed for Old Inlet. They slipped past Fort Caswell and the outer batteries guarding the harbor without being seen. The *Raleigh* wasn't in the harbor. Cushing was determined to find her, even if it meant rowing all the way up the Cape Fear River to Wilmington, some thirty miles from where he had started.

The moon had long been up by the time they reached Fort Anderson, about twelve miles from the inlet on the west bank of the river. Rebel soldiers spotted them as they passed by in the moonlit channel and opened fire with rifle muskets. Cushing turned downstream, and when the boat got far enough away, he cut across the river and headed back upstream, hoping to send any pursuing enemy boats on a wild goose chase downriver.

It was nearly dawn by the time they got within seven miles of Wilmington. Cushing and his men landed, hauled the boat well ashore, covered it with tree branches, and hid in the bushes. The hiding place afforded Cushing a good view of the river. Throughout the course of the day he saw nine steamers pass by, but no sign of the ironclad. Three of the vessels were sleek blockade-runners. Cushing suppressed an urge to try to stop them.

Just after dusk, two small boats rounded a point near the Yankees' hiding place. Cushing figured the occupants were soldiers out searching for him. He arrayed his men behind a log, walked out from behind the bushes, and ordered the intruders to surrender. The startled boaters turned out not to be a search party of soldiers, but civilians on a fishing trip. They told Cushing that the *Raleigh* had run on a river bar at high water. As the tide had fallen, the weight of the armor had split open her bottom. The ironclad was now a wreck, not a threat to the blockaders.

Cushing figured that as long as he was this close to Wilmington, he might as well take a look at the city's defenses, especially since he knew that plans were afoot in Washington for a campaign against Wilmington. That night he and the men boarded their cutter and the fishermen's boats and, taking the fishermen along at gunpoint as guides, rowed up near the city. After examining the lay of the harbor and its obstructions, they rowed down to Mott's Creek, a small tributary of the Cape Fear River about four miles below Wilmington. Leaving half the men to guard the boats, Cushing led the other half to a hiding spot along the main road into town. "We were now just outside of the rebel city in the midst of swarms of soldiers and lines of fortifications and it was policy to keep very quiet," Cushing later recalled, "but we were growing hungry and a little cross and did not long suffer people to pass unmolested."[19]

Two civilians on their way home from a fishing trip happened by. The Yankee sailors jumped them. One of them turned out to be the owner of a nearby country store. Soon, a lone horseman approached. The Yankee sailors jumped him. He turned out to be a Confederate Army mail carrier, whose bag contained some two hundred letters and documents describing life at Fort Fisher, but which were not terribly revealing about the defenses.

To settle the grumbling from the sailors' stomachs, William Howorth donned the mail carrier's gray uniform, pocketed some Confederate money from letters in his mail bag, mounted his horse, and set out for the shopkeeper's store to buy some food. He returned with chickens, eggs, and milk that, together with blackberries growing nearby, "formed a meal that could not be improved in Seceshia," as Cushing recalled, "and left us ready for anything."[20] While the men were preparing the meal, Howorth turned to the storekeeper. "I informed your wife that I'd met you down the road," he said, "and that you directed me to tell Lizzy to give me the best she had. I paid for what I got, so you needn't worry on that score."[21]

Over the course of the day, Cushing and his party of eight accumulated some two dozen civilian prisoners. As evening approached Cushing decided to send his men and the prisoners back to the boats while he waited by the road to capture the evening mail carrier from Wilmington, who, as one of the prisoners said, should be along at any moment. Sure enough the mailman and another horseman appeared just as the Yankees were herding the prisoners across the road. The mail carrier took one look at the blue uniforms, wheeled about, and rode hell bent for leather back toward Wilmington. Cushing chased them for a while, but they had a good head start and got away.

Cushing decided he'd better get while the getting was good. After cutting the telegraph wires running along the road, he led his men and prisoners back to the Cape Fear River. He put the prisoners in the fishermen's boats and towed them out into the river with the cutter. He intended to leave most of them on an uninhabited island in the middle of the waterway.

Darkness had fallen, and the boats had just reached the island when a steamer rounded the point and seemed to come straight at them. Cushing ordered everyone overboard, shoved the boats in among some marsh grass, and had the men hide behind them, threatening to kill any prisoner who made a noise. In the darkness the steamer passed within ten feet of the Yankees without her crew seeing them.

When the steamer had gone, Cushing removed the sails and oars from the fishermen's boats, put twenty of the prisoners in them, and set them adrift in the tideway, figuring they'd be picked up in the morning. It would be faster than trying to land them, he reasoned. One of the prisoners he kept was a river pilot. Cushing forced the waterman to show him the wreck of the *Raleigh* to confirm the fishermen's story. It checked out. Cushing paused to leave a note on a buoy for a Confederate colonel who had vowed that the Yankee would never again enter the river, then started on the long pull downstream.

After passing Fort Anderson, the Yankees captured a boat with four Rebel soldiers and two civilians on board. From them Cushing learned that a guard boat with seventy-five soldiers was lying in wait downstream near the New Inlet entrance to the river. Cushing determined to try and capture the guard boat and make for the sea in it.

The Yankee cutter had closed to within fifteen yards of the guard boat when nine other Rebel boats under oars and one under sail suddenly appeared. Cushing feinted this way and that, eventually managing to outmaneuver his pursuers and make good his escape through New Inlet. By the time his cutter reached the fleet shortly after dawn on June 26, he had gone sixty-eight hours without sleep.

Cushing's second foray into the Cape Fear River was even more daring than his first, although some said it was equally unproductive. Gideon Welles, who was never among the naysayers, sent Cushing another letter of commendation on behalf of the Navy Department. Welles also commended Howorth and Jones and awarded the Medal of Honor to three of Cushing's sailors. Meanwhile, Cushing returned to cruising for prizes.

The next time Cushing came to the attention of the secretary of the Navy, it was not for a stunning feat of arms, but a stunning breach of international law. Five days after Cushing returned from the Cape Fear River, lookouts on the *Monticello* sighted a small brig. Cushing, who was doing paperwork in his cabin, gave the usual orders to board the vessel and check her papers. The brig was hailed, but she gave no answer and kept going. Instead of the usual practice of showing the colors and firing a blank round, the crew of the *Monticello* fired two or three musket shots across her bow. The brig hove to. She proved to be the British merchantman *Hound.* The *Monticello* sent over a boarding party. Enraged at the firing of live rounds near his men, the master of the *Hound* swore profusely at the boarding officer. His papers checked out, however, and the *Hound* was allowed to proceed.

The boarding officer made his report upon returning to the *Monticello.* Cushing, enraged by the British skipper's rude behavior, stormed out of his cabin to the quarterdeck and overhauled the *Hound* once again. This time, Cushing had her master and his papers brought on board the *Monticello.* He detained the master for hours, made him apologize to the boarding officer, then sent him on his way.

Cushing had always been a bit haughty and highhanded in his treatment of merchant skippers, and the Navy Department had already received several complaints about him, but this time he had gone too far. The master of the *Hound* filed a formal complaint with her majesty's government. The British minister in Washington, in turn, protested to Secretary of State William Seward. Welles demanded an explanation from Cushing. The young officer justified his actions on the basis that the skipper of the *Hound* had failed to treat a "national ship" with proper respect.[22]

Instead of praising Cushing, Welles censured him for firing live rounds, stopping the *Hound* a second time after already determining her to be on a legitimate voyage, and detaining her master "unlawfully and unnecessarily." "The Department fails to find in your explanation any excuse for your disregard of international law and courtesy," the secretary fumed, "but regrets to perceive in your conduct a disregard of either, and a flagrant violation of its oft-repeated instructions." Welles acknowledged that the British skipper had indeed behaved discourteously, but asserted that Cushing had no right to detain him or assume temporary authority over his vessel. It was an abuse of the belligerent right of search. "I must enjoin you to be more cautious in future," Welles concluded. "Such proceedings repeated can not fail to bring upon you the serious displeasure of your Government and result to your regret and injury. While the Department is always ready to accord to officers of the service, as it has in several instances in your own case, due credit for valor and efficiency in the discharge of duty, it is not the less so to disapprove and punish when disapprobation and punishment are deserved."[23]

Two days later, Welles wrote Seward that Cushing's conduct in the case of the *Hound* was unjustified. "Lieutenant Cushing is quite young," Welles noted, "which fact may be pleaded in extenuation of his improper conduct. The Department regrets the occurrence and hopes . . . that the action it has taken may be satisfactory to the injured parties."[24] This closed the book on the incident.

Cushing quickly shook off the rebuke and began planning a new mission, one that would result in his greatest feat of arms— the destruction of the Confederate ironclad *Albemarle.* In the spring of 1864, the *Albemarle* stood second only to the CSS *Virginia* in the amount of damage inflicted by a Rebel ironclad on the U.S. Navy.

The Confederates built the *Albemarle* in a cornfield on the Roanoke River west of Plymouth, North Carolina. Laid down early in 1863, she measured 152 feet long, drew eight feet of water, and bore the usual floating mansard roof appearance of Rebel ironclads. Armed with an iron-tipped ram and two rifled cannons, she could beat any available Union ship with a shallow enough draft to operate in the North Carolina sounds. Rear Admiral Lee had repeatedly urged General Butler, commander of the Department of Virginia and North Carolina, to attack the *Albemarle*'s construction site. Although Butler had the men to do it, Army forces in North Carolina refused to budge unless escorted by the Navy. Since the site lay too far upstream in shallow water for Union ships to operate safely, the Confederates finished the *Albemarle* unmolested.

In the spring of 1864, the Confederates unleashed the ironclad and 7,000 men on Plymouth. Against this onslaught the Union mustered 3,000 troops and the gunboats *Miami, Southfield, Ceres,* and *Whitehead* under Cushing's old friend Charles Flusser. At 3:30 A.M. on April 19, the *Albemarle* attacked the Union flotilla in the Roanoke River defending Plymouth. Flusser had the wooden double-enders *Miami* and *Southfield* lashed together with a hawser in hopes that he could handle them as one ship and trap the *Albemarle* in between them. He stood to meet the Rebel ironclad with guns blazing. While Union shells caromed harmlessly off the *Albemarle*'s armor, the ironclad rammed and sank the *Southfield* and drove off the other ships. A fragment of a projectile Flusser fired ricocheted off the ironclad and killed him instantly. With support from the *Albemarle,* Rebel soldiers took Plymouth later that day.

Union forces subsequently withdrew from Washington and the Confederates planned another attack on New Bern. On May 5, the Rebel ram moved out, steaming into Albemarle Sound. This time she faced four double-enders and four smaller wooden gunboats. A fierce fight ensued. Some 280 Union projectiles struck the *Albemarle,* killing one man. The ironclad's gunfire killed eight Union sailors, wounded twenty-one, and disabled the double-ender *Sassacus,* but the Union flotilla drove her off. The ram steamed back up the Roanoke River to Plymouth.

Although the naval battle ended in a draw, the Confederate thrust against New Bern failed without support from the *Albemarle.* Stalemate descended onto eastern North Carolina. For the next several months, the Confederate ironclad remained docked at Plymouth, where she continued to pose a threat to Union naval forces in eastern North Carolina, while a flotilla from the North Atlantic Blockading Squadron remained on station at the river's mouth in case she reappeared.

Rear Admiral Lee wanted nothing more than to destroy the *Albemarle.* He weighed his options. Monitors drew too much water to get over the bar into Albemarle Sound. He didn't want to risk any more wooden ships in face-to-face combat with the ironclad. A small-boat raid seemed the best option. And nobody was better suited to lead such a raid than Cushing.

Lee summoned Cushing to the flagship. Cushing arrived on July 5 and reported to the admiral in his cabin. Lee told Cushing that he wanted him to lead an expedition to destroy the *Albemarle.* Cushing proposed attacking the ironclad with gunboats, but Lee said that that was out. Cushing then came up with two alternatives for small boat raids. The first involved carrying inflatable rubber boats across the swamp behind Plymouth, dropping the boats in the river a few hundred yards from the *Albemarle,* and attacking her with a torpedo. The second involved attacking the ironclad with "a light-draft, rifle-proof, swift steam barge, fitted with a torpedo," as Lee put it to Gideon Welles.[25] Cushing preferred the latter, using two boats. "I intended that one boat should dash in while the other stood by to throw canister and renew the attempt if the first failed."[26]

The plan was so bold that Lee wouldn't authorize it without higher authority. He ordered Cushing to go to Washington to submit the plan to the Navy Department in person. Gus Fox didn't think the idea would work, but he figured it was worth a try.

Fox ordered Cushing to New York to purchase suitable vessels. Cushing wrote in his memoirs:

Finding some boats building for picket duty, I selected two and proceeded to fit them out. They were open launches about thirty feet in length with small engines propelled by a screw. A twelve-pounder howitzer was fitted to the bows of each and a boom rigged out, some fourteen feet in length, swinging by a goose-neck hinge to the bluff of the bow. A topping lift to a stanchion inboard raised or lowered it and the torpedo was fitted into an iron slide at the end. This was intended to be detached from the boom by means of a heel jigger leading inboard and exploded by another line connecting with a pin which held a grape shot over nipple and cap.[27]

While the boats were being readied, Cushing practiced with the complicated boom arrangement and successfully exploded several torpedoes in the Hudson River. The arrangement didn't inspire confidence, however. "It has many defects," he noted in his memoirs, "and I would not again attempt its use."[28]

The boats were ready by mid-September. They departed from New York on September 22, with Acting Ens. William Howorth in command of *Picket Boat No. 1* and Acting Ens. Andrew Stockholm in command of *Picket Boat No. 2*.

While the boats steamed southward, Cushing detoured northward to Fredonia, planning to rejoin the boats at Fort Monroe. After all, he reasoned, it might well be his last chance to visit home. He called on relatives and friends, making his entrance into one family's kitchen on horseback, and flirted with a local girl. As the time for his departure drew near, he got serious. Although the operation against the *Albemarle* remained a closely guarded secret, Cushing couldn't resist telling his mother about it. He laid out the full details, sparing her none of the danger involved. "If I do not succeed," he is supposed to have said, "you will have no Will Cushing."[29] There is no detailed account of her reaction to news that her youngest son was about to embark on what must have seemed like a suicide mission a year after she had lost Allie, but she certainly feared for Will's life. The next day Cushing began making his way to Fort Monroe.

Meanwhile, the picket boats steamed to Baltimore via the Chesapeake and Delaware Canal, then headed down the bay. Although both boats had engine trouble on the way, they reached Point Lookout at the mouth of the Potomac River on October 7. Howorth pressed on with *No. 1* to Fort Monroe while Stockholm spent the night repairing *No. 2*'s engine. Stockholm got underway the next morning, but the engine soon broke down again. He made harbor at the mouth of Reason Creek in the Great Wicomico Bay. These were Virginia waters. A unit of Confederate home guardsmen came upon the boat and opened fire. Stockholm slipped the cable and tried to escape, but *Picket Boat No. 2* ran aground. After expending all his ammunition in a fierce firefight, Stockholm destroyed the boat and surrendered. "This was a great misfortune and I have never understood how so stupid a thing occurred," Cushing ranted in his memoirs. "I forget the name of the volunteer ensign to whose care it was entrusted, but am pleased to know that he was taken prisoner. I trust that his bed was not of down or his food that of princes while in rebel hands."[30]

Cushing arrived at Fort Monroe on October 10. Howorth and *No. 1* were already there, but Cushing didn't yet know what fate had befallen Stockholm and anxiously awaited his arrival.

Two days later, Rear Adm. David Dixon Porter relieved Rear Admiral Lee as commander of the North Atlantic Blockading Squadron. By the fall of 1864, with the Mississippi River under Union control and Charleston and Mobile effectively sealed off from the outside world, Wilmington remained the last Confederate port open to blockade-runners. Gideon Welles lobbied Lincoln for a joint Army-Navy campaign to capture Wilmington. The president liked the idea, but left the final decision up to his general in chief. Ulysses S. Grant approved it also, but on the condition that Welles replace Admiral Lee. Why Grant wanted Lee sacked is unclear, and although Welles did not relish the idea, he went along with it. The secretary thought Lee had served faithfully and intelligently, but considered him overcautious. When Welles offered command of the North Atlantic Blockading Squadron to David Dixon Porter, the mercurial, but capable, officer accepted it.

Grant believed Porter to be as great an admiral as Lord Nelson. Sixteen months after entering the war as a lieutenant, Porter assumed command of the Mississippi Squadron as an acting rear admiral. His crowning achievement was the naval support he provided to Grant during the campaign that brought down Vicksburg by July 4, 1863. Porter and Grant respected one another deeply, and as partners in command, they had formed one of the Civil War's most effective joint teams. Witty, energetic, audacious, acerbic, ambitious, prone to exaggeration and braggadocio, blunt to the point of imprudence, and blessed with a photographic memory and a keenly analytical mind, Porter stood behind only Farragut in the pantheon of Civil War naval heroes.

It is not known what Cushing thought of Porter, but Porter didn't think much of Cushing at this juncture. The admiral regarded the lieutenant as an impetuous daredevil who had more luck than common sense and whose feats were "more daring than important."[31] He was doubtless fuming with Cushing for frolicking in Fredonia while Stockholm was stumbling about with *Picket Boat No. 2*. On the day after he took command of the squadron, he sent Cushing off in an Army tug to look for the missing boat.

Things nearly got a lot worse. On October 19, Gideon Welles received word over the telegraph that the Rebels had captured *Picket Boat No. 2*. The secretary immediately fired off an angry message to Cushing at Hampton Roads:

> Why was this boat separated from the others, and have you given your personal attendance to getting those vessels to Hampton Roads? A full report of your proceedings from the time you left New York is required. The Department has been almost in total ignorance of your movements and action since you have been on special duty, and what it has learned concerning the progress of the boats towards their destination has been through orders. You have not replied to the Department's letter of September 14th, in relation to allegations that you improperly disposed of certain articles belonging to the schooner *James Douglass* [the abandoned schooner he had found loaded with rotten coconuts and bananas], and inflicted illegal punishments while on board the *Monticello*; nor has the Depart-

ment yet been able to obtain a report from you of the picking up of the schooner above mentioned.[32]

Once again, Cushing's career seemed on the line.

Fortunately for Cushing's future in the Navy, Welles's message arrived at Hampton Roads after he had already left. Upon returning from his fruitless search for *No. 2,* Cushing begged Porter to allow him to undertake the mission with the remaining launch. Porter granted the request and promised Cushing a promotion if he succeeded, but he wasn't sanguine about the outcome. "I have no great confidence in his success," he wrote Comdr. William H. Macomb, senior naval officer, Sounds of North Carolina, "but you will afford him all the assistance in your power, and keep boats ready to pick him up in case of failure." Porter wasn't trying to get rid of Cushing; he was trying to get rid of the *Albemarle.* According to Porter's orders, if the ironclad appeared, Macomb was to "make a dash at her with every vessel you have" and board her, "even if half your vessels are sunk."[33]

On or about October 15,[34] Cushing embarked on *Picket Boat No. 1* with Howorth and six other men, departing Hampton Roads for Albemarle Sound by way of the Chesapeake and Albemarle Canal through the Dismal Swamp. On October 24, they reached the mouth of the Roanoke River and Cushing reported to Commander Macomb on board his flagship, the double-ender gunboat *Shamrock.* The lieutenant asked for more men. When word got out that Cushing was seeking volunteers for a secret mission, volunteers poured out of the woodwork, some even offering a month's pay for the chance. Macomb picked six of the best men. Cushing assembled these sailors along with Howorth and the six sailors who had accompanied him on the launch and explained what he intended to do. He gave them a chance to decline the mission. Every one volunteered to go without hesitation, for none wanted to miss out on a chance for glory.

Acting Assistant Paymaster Francis H. Swan, one of the volunteers, later recalled Cushing on the eve of his greatest moment:

He was a young man about twenty-one years of age, tall, very erect, with light brown hair flowing down to his shoulders. His interest though in all that was going on around him and his geniality attracted everyone on board. His exploits on the coast of North Carolina had preceded him, and he was fully up in style and manner to the picture we had drawn of him. . . . He was in excellent spirits and inspired general enthusiasm.[35]

Cushing spent the next two days making final preparations. He talked at length with Acting Ens. Rudolph Sommers, who earlier had made several small-boat reconnaissances of the *Albemarle*. The ram was moored along the Plymouth waterfront, Sommers said. The town lay eight miles upriver. The waterway averaged 150 to 200 yards wide between Plymouth and the fleet. As many as 4,000 soldiers defended the town. The half-submerged wreck of the *Southfield*, sunk in the engagement with the *Albemarle*, lay in the middle of the river about a mile below Plymouth. The Rebels were using her as a picket station. Cushing decided he was ready. Sommers begged to go. Cushing admired his pluck, but turned him down, for Sommers was so exhausted from his last foray into the river that he could barely walk.

On the night of October 26, Cushing got the picket boat underway and headed up the Roanoke, but had to abort the attempt when the launch ran aground. Although he lost a day, he gained an extra volunteer, Acting Master's Mate Thomas S. Gay, who jokingly offered Cushing ten thousand dollars if he let him participate in the mission. Cushing allowed Gay to join the crew, even though he didn't have the money. The next morning, the fleet rescued three escaped slaves swimming in the river. The slaves told Cushing that the Rebels had posted some twenty-five soldiers on the *Southfield*. Cushing figured he'd tow one of the *Shamrock*'s cutters to the wreck, then cast it off to deal with the pickets while the launch proceeded upstream. He needed eleven more men to man the cutter. When an officer of the *Shamrock* mustered the crew and asked for volunteers, the entire crew stepped forward. Two officers and ten men were selected. Cushing would try again after dark.

The night of October 27, 1864 was cloudy and rainy, but warm, about 65 degrees, with a water temperature of about 55 degrees. At about 11:30 P.M. Cushing reached the mouth of the Roanoke. *Picket Boat No. 1* steamed slowly and quietly upriver close to the south bank, under cover of darkness, rain, and overhanging trees, its noise muffled by a tarpaulin stuffed inside the walls of a box built around the engine, which also concealed the light from its boiler fire. For more than three hours the fourteen men in the launch and the twelve men in the cutter dealt with their fears in silence. They passed within twenty or thirty yards of the schooner described by the escaped slaves and the wreck of the *Southfield,* but none of the Rebel pickets spotted them. One of the options Cushing had considered was to board the *Albemarle* and "take her alive," as he put it in his memoirs, and, having gotten this far without being discovered, he was seriously entertaining the notion.[36]

At about 3 A.M., Rebel pickets on board the *Albemarle* spotted the launch, hailed its crew, and sounded the alarm. So much for boarding. Cushing cast off the cutter and made for the ram under a full head of steam. Rebels on board ship and on shore started shooting and lit a bonfire, but it was more effective in illuminating the ironclad for Cushing than illuminating the launch for the Rebels. The flickering light revealed the ram made fast to a wharf, with a pen of logs around her about thirty feet from her side.

Cushing steamed past the ironclad, then circled about and headed straight for the log boom. Rebel small-arms fire peppered the launch and wounded a sailor. The air seemed alive with bullets. Buckshot tore away the back of Cushing's coat and a bullet carried away the sole of a shoe. Swan recalled that Cushing actually laughed at his predicament. The Rebels hailed the launch again, demanding to know what boat it was. The men replied with comical answers. Cushing replied with a dose of canister from the boat gun that bounced off the armor of the ram and peppered the men ashore, suppressing their fire for a brief interval.

The launch hit the boom at full speed, drove the logs toward the ironclad for a moment, then the bow reared up as the boat passed partway over a log and hung there, right in front of one of the *Albemarle*'s 6.4-inch rifled cannons. Cushing stood in the launch's bow, holding the torpedo release line in his right hand and the trigger pin line in his left hand, while four bullets tore into his clothing and countless others buzzed by. Somehow the crew managed to lower the boom, and the boat drove the boom and torpedo under the ram. The Rebels demanded their surrender.

"Leave the ram," Cushing yelled, "or I'll blow you to pieces!"[37]

Cushing could hear the gun captain on the *Albemarle* issuing orders to the crew above the shouts of the Confederate soldiers ashore and the din of their firing. He raced to detonate the torpedo before they fired the cannon. Even as a bullet grazed his left hand, Cushing coolly counted to five while the torpedo rose into position, then pulled the trigger pin line. The roar of simultaneous explosions filled his ears. The round from the ironclad's cannon flew overhead. The torpedo threw up an immense column of water, which almost swamped the launch. But it also blew a six-foot-wide hole in the bottom of the ram.

Again the Rebels demanded that Cushing surrender.

Again, Cushing refused. "Men, save yourselves!" he shouted, then he flung off his sword, revolver, and the remains of his coat and shoes, dove into the water, and swam toward the middle of the river.[38] Bullets and grapeshot splashed around him like handfuls of gravel flung into the water as he put distance between himself and the enemy soldiers on shore. The cold water, the drag of his clothing, and the effort to get away drained his strength. Rebels with torches appeared in small boats to hunt for survivors. Cushing didn't know for sure whether the ram had sunk, and he soon lost track of his men. About a half mile from town, he encountered a sailor struggling in the river, but Cushing was too weakened to save him, and the man slipped under the murky water and drowned. Of the fourteen men who had accompanied Cushing in the launch, two drowned, eleven were captured, including the ubiquitous Howorth, and one made good his escape. The crew of the cutter, meanwhile, captured the pickets posted on the wreck of the *Southfield*. After hearing the sounds of battle and not seeing any sign of their comrades, they concluded that Cushing and his men were lost and returned downriver to the fleet.

Cushing, meanwhile, kept swimming. "There was a determination not to sink, a will not to give up," he noted in his memoirs, "and I kept up a sort of mechanical motion long after my bodily force was in fact expended."[39] At last Cushing touched mud, rose, took a step, then fell. Too exhausted to move, he remained where he lay, half in the water and half in the mud, until daylight.

Dawn on October 28 found Cushing in a swamp east of Plymouth, about forty yards from a Rebel fortification. Like a cold-blooded animal's, Cushing's strength returned with the growing light and heat from the sun. The fort was a beehive of activity, and Cushing took comfort in having set the bees buzzing.

Cushing noticed a dry fringe of rushes at the edge of the swamp near where he lay. If he could get to it, he figured, he could escape. But thirty or forty feet of open ground lay between him and the rushes, all within sight of a sentry walking the parapet in the Rebel fort. When the sentry turned for a moment, Cushing sprang up and started running. He got halfway to the rushes when the sentry turned back again. Cushing dropped to the ground between two paths and remained motionless, the mud enabling him to blend in. While waiting for another chance to make a break for it, four soldiers passed by, one nearly stepping on his arm. They were talking about the sinking of the *Albemarle*, wondering how it was done.

After they passed, Cushing gave up on the idea of getting to the rushes. He dug his heels and elbows into the ground and slithered back into the swamp on his belly. Hours passed and he crept along, with thorns and briars tearing into his flesh. He crawled past a working party of Rebel soldiers, through a cornfield, and into a patch of woods, where he encountered an old black man. Cushing offered the fellow twenty dollars in greenbacks and some texts of scripture if he would go into town and bring back news of the ram. The man struck out for Plymouth while Cushing rested. The slave soon returned bearing the welcome news that the *Albemarle* had indeed gone down.

Cushing resumed his journey through the swamp. At about 2 P.M. he stumbled onto a road, which led him to a picket station by a creek, where he found a small skiff tied to the root of a cypress tree. When the soldiers manning the station sat down to eat, Cushing slipped into the water, cast loose the skiff, and, keeping the boat between him and the soldiers, drifted downstream until he rounded a bend. Then he slid into the boat and began paddling. Hours and miles passed and darkness fell. At last Cushing reached the mouth of the Roanoke and the open sound. He kept paddling till he came upon the *Valley City,* one of the vessels on picket duty at the mouth of the river. Cushing hailed the gunboat, then fell back into the skiff, exhausted. The *Valley City* lowered boats to investigate and Cushing was soon on board, where he was given some brandy and water. It was near midnight.

Word of Cushing's return and success spread through the flotilla like wildfire. Union sailors cheered and fired off rockets in celebration. Officers immediately laid plans for retaking Plymouth, now that the Rebels lacked naval support, and did so on October 31. Meanwhile, the *Valley City* took Cushing to Hampton Roads, where he reported to Admiral Porter in person.

Porter had already heard of Cushing's success. If he still harbored doubts about the young officer, he kept them to himself. He issued a general order describing Cushing's feat to be read to the officers and men of each ship in the squadron: "Lieutenant William B. Cushing has displayed a heroic enterprise seldom equaled and never excelled. . . . The gallant exploits of Lieutenant Cushing previous to this affair will form a bright page in the history of the war, but they have all been eclipsed by the destruction of the Albemarle."[40]

Indeed, Cushing became an instant national hero. Gideon Welles's ire at the loss of *Picket Boat No. 2* vanished. He sent

Cushing yet another letter of commendation from the Navy Department. Abraham Lincoln recommended Cushing for a vote
of thanks. Congress passed the vote on December 20, a higher
accolade in those days than the Medal of Honor. Cushing was
promoted to lieutenant commander, becoming the youngest of
that rank in the Navy. His own account of the destruction of the
Albemarle appeared in many Northern newspapers. Testimonials
and praise poured in from the New York Chamber of Commerce, the Union League of Philadelphia, and numerous other
organizations and individuals. People clamored for his photo-
graph. Politicians jostled each other to be seen in public with
him. Someone dubbed him "Albemarle" Cushing. The nickname stuck.

Meanwhile, Cushing was granted an extended leave. He
headed home in early November. People showered him with
congratulations all along the way. The citizens of Fredonia gathered in the concert hall and greeted him with a standing ovation
and round after round of cheering. No doubt Mary Cushing was
relieved that her son had survived and thrilled that he had succeeded. But she was still his mother. "Ah, Willie, beware of
pride," she allegedly admonished, "for many is the time I have
put you to bed while I mended your only suit of clothes."[41]
Cushing stayed home for a week, then went on a tour of Northern cities making speeches and reveling in the limelight.

Chapter 5

Final Rays of Glory

WHILE CUSHING WAS BASKING in the adulation, Porter was planning the Civil War's last great joint operation, the campaign against Wilmington. Cushing didn't want to miss out, so he returned to duty after Thanksgiving. Porter put him in temporary command of his flagship, the USS *Malvern*.

Much to Porter's dismay, Ben Butler would be leading the Army forces assigned to the Wilmington expedition. Porter and Butler had become bitter enemies in 1862 during the New Orleans campaign when Butler took what Porter considered undue credit for the capture of the Crescent City. As a result of their enmity, the admiral and general spent as little time together as possible while planning operations against Wilmington.

The key to Wilmington was Fort Fisher, built near the northern and more frequently used entrance into the Cape Fear River at New Inlet. Situated at the tip of Confederate Point, a long, narrow peninsula that formed the east bank of the Cape Fear River, Fort Fisher resembled the number seven, with its elbow pointing northeast. The short bar faced north to defend against an attack by land from up the peninsula. It measured 480 yards and contained nineteen heavy guns and two mortars behind log-and-sand breastworks overlooking a minefield and a nine-foot-high palisade. The elbow towered thirty-two feet above the beach. The long arm of the seven faced the sea and stretched 1,300 yards. It consisted of a series of sand, turf, and log batteries, which, when viewed from the Atlantic, resembled a row of haystacks connected by walls. Twenty-four heavy cannon in the long-arm batteries faced the sea. The garrison numbered between eight hundred and fifteen hundred men, with varying numbers of additional troops available from Wilmington. By late 1864, Fort Fisher and Charleston were the Confederacy's most intensely fortified pieces of coastline.

The plan for what came to be called the first Fort Fisher expedition, or Butler's expedition, was simple. While the fleet bombarded Fort Fisher from the Atlantic, troops would land north of the fort, then move southward to carry Fort Fisher in a frontal assault. If the assault failed, the troops were to dig in for a siege, cutting off the fort with a line of entrenchments across the peninsula.

The North Atlantic Blockading Squadron opened fire early in the afternoon on Christmas Eve 1864. By nightfall, the fleet had fired some 10,000 rounds at the defenses, but many Union gunners concentrated their fire on the rebel flags and shot after shot went screeching right over the fort. The cannonade inflicted only minor damage on Fort Fisher, and there were only twenty-three casualties among its defenders. Meanwhile, Butler's men began landing above the fort. On Christmas day the fleet resumed the bombardment.

Porter wanted to run some double-enders through New Inlet into the Cape Fear River to bombard Fort Fisher from behind, but the channel wasn't where the chart said it was. Cushing volunteered to find the channel and to check for torpedoes. Porter assented.

Cushing, another officer, and twelve men loaded the *Malvern's* first cutter with grappling irons, lead lines, and buoys. At about 12:30 or 1:00 P.M. on Christmas afternoon, the boat stood in toward the shore, flying the blue and white pennant of a commanding officer. Cushing sat in the stern, decked out in all the gold braid his rank entitled him to wear, while a sailor stood in the bow heaving a sounding lead and calling out the depth. "For ten minutes the rebels seemed paralyzed with this audacious piece of coast surveying," a reporter later wrote, "and then they trained their guns on the boat and fired."[1]

Boats from other vessels moved in to assist. The Yankees discovered several torpedoes and marked them with buoys. A Rebel solid shot struck one of the boats, killing a sailor and sending the boat to the bottom, but the other boats rescued the survivors.

Cushing, meanwhile, moved closer and closer to the fort, oblivious to the shot and shell flying about. Near misses threw up jets of water that splashed his men. When he got close enough that "a biscuit might be tossed from the boat to the beach," as the reporter put it, "Cushing signaled his men to cease rowing, and he stood up in the stern of his frail craft and took a cool and deliberate survey of the fort."[2] Near misses threw so much water in the boat that Cushing and his men had to bail. He spent some six hours in the cutter defying death and marking what Porter described as "a very narrow and crooked channel."[3] The admiral decided not to risk sending any ships over the bar.

Meanwhile, Maj. Gen. Godfrey Weitzel, an engineer, determined that the naval bombardment had inflicted almost no damage on Fort Fisher. He reported to Butler that an infantry assault would be suicidal. Butler concurred. After receiving word of the approach of a Confederate division from Wilmington, Butler decided to withdraw instead of digging in as Grant had ordered.

On December 27, Porter detached Cushing from the flagship and returned him to command of the *Monticello,* on station off Old Inlet. Cushing was glad to be free of duty as the admiral's chauffeur. He had no sooner stepped on board the *Monticello* than the ship destroyed a blockade-runner.

Meanwhile, Lincoln sacked Butler for his failure to follow orders. Porter sent dispatches to the Navy Department requesting that the troops be sent back to Fort Fisher under a new commander. Welles and Fox lobbied Lincoln for a second expedition. Sherman, whose army had recently reached the sea at Savannah, proposed attacking Wilmington in the course of marching his army through the Carolinas toward Virginia. Grant figured that Wilmington would make a good point for supplying Sherman, so he approved a second expedition, with Maj. Gen. Alfred Howe Terry leading the troops.

The second expedition departed Hampton Roads on January 6, 1865. Terry commanded some 9,600 men; Porter's fleet numbered fifty-eight ships with 396 guns. Storms delayed their arrival off Fort Fisher until late in the afternoon of the twelfth. Some 1,500 Confederates manned Fort Fisher, while a division of some 6,424 infantry and cavalry occupied the peninsula north of the fort.

On January 13, some 8,000 Union troops landed above Fort Fisher under the cover of a naval bombardment and dug in between the fort and the rebel division to the north. The entire fleet reopened on Fort Fisher mid-morning on January 14. This time, the ships concentrated their fire on the enemy's guns. By the end of the day, the Rebels had lost all but three or four of their land-face cannon and at least two hundred killed and wounded, some 13 percent of the garrison.

On the evening of January 14, General Terry rowed out to meet with Admiral Porter on the *Malvern*. They hammered out a plan calling for Union forces to bombard Fort Fisher until 3 P.M. the next afternoon, then Terry would signal Porter to shift the fleet's fire from the fort's land face to its sea face. At that moment, a column of about 3,200 troops would assault the west end of the land face, approaching the fort by the road from Wilmington. To the east, a volunteer force of 2,261 sailors and marines under Capt. Kidder Randolph Breese, Porter's fleet captain, would attack the northeast bastion at the angle of the seven. Naturally, Cushing determined to join the naval assault, leading a detachment of sailors.

At 2 P.M. on the afternoon of January 15, Cushing stepped ashore to join the naval brigade. He had a reunion of sorts with old friends from Annapolis, Ben Porter and Sam Preston, each slated to lead a detachment from the fleet. "Preston had a reputation for courage," historians Roske and Van Doren write of the meeting. "But when Cushing and Porter found him he looked reflective, his long features were unusually solemn.

"'Cushing,' he said, 'I have a prophetic feeling that I am not coming out alive.'

"'Nonsense,' said Porter. 'You bet *I* am.'

"'Cheer up, Preston,' Cushing said, 'and let's drink to success and little Nell.' Little Nell was Ellen Grosvenor, popular with all the Cushings and their friends, and later the wife of Milton Cushing. Cushing took a bottle of beer out of his pocket, which he opened and passed around, and they all drank the toast— 'Success, and little Nell.' "[4]

Cushing and his friends parted, formed up their men, and steeled themselves for the assault. Armed with cutlasses and pistols, the sailors were to "board" the fort under cover of musket fire from the Marines.

Finally, at 3:25 P.M., the ships ceased fire and blew their steam whistles. The sailors stood up, gave a cheer, and charged, running down the beach toward the most strongly defended part of Fort Fisher. The Marines, who were to provide covering fire with rifle muskets, didn't advance far enough forward to support the sailors. The defenders greeted them with a hail of cannon and small-arms fire. The blue-clad column halted in confusion about fifty yards from the palisade in front of the fort. Cushing watched Ben Porter grab a flag, urge the men forward, and fall, shot through the chest. "Carry me down the beach," he ordered. Four sailors picked him up, but two were shot dead. Porter waved the others off, then died himself. Cushing turned to see how Preston was faring, only to witness his friend's premonition of death come true as he fell with a bullet through his skull.

Cushing tried to rally the men and urge them forward, charging ahead himself. When he got through the palisade, he turned back around, only to discover that few had followed him. He dropped down onto the sand for cover. "Captain Cushing!"

shouted one of his men. "They are retreating, sir!" Cushing looked back again and saw the column break, the sailors running away as fast as fear would carry them.

"I made up my mind that it was my duty to join my men and rally them," Cushing recalled. "That retreat was a fearful sight. The dead lay thickly strewn along the beach, and the wounded falling constantly called for help to their comrades and prayed to God that they might not be left behind. I saw the wounded stagger to their feet all weak and bloody, only to receive other and more fatal wounds, and fall to rise no more."[5]

Cushing helped the fallen, dragging wounded sailors to higher ground before the incoming tide drowned them. Late in the afternoon General Terry saw him rallying men to renew the assault. Thinking it would be suicide, Terry ordered the attack stopped before it started. He directed Cushing and his men to man the Army entrenchments against a counterattack he expected from the rebel division to the north. The sailors did so. The counterattack never materialized and Cushing returned to the fleet the next morning.

Determined to stop the naval brigade before the sailors reached the northeast bastion, the Rebels had concentrated their fire on the sailors, killing and wounding about three hundred of them. Whether intentional or not, the diversion enabled the Army column to reach the fort relatively unscathed. By the time the defenders realized that Union soldiers had gotten into the fort, it was too late. A vicious fight ensued, but the Yankees overwhelmed the outnumbered rebels, who surrendered at about 10 P.M. When word of the victory reached the fleet, the sailors filled the sky with fireworks.

Cushing spent January 16 clearing torpedoes in the waters near the fort. Early the next morning, the crew of the *Monticello* heard explosions and saw a large fire in the vicinity of Fort Caswell across the harbor at Old Inlet. Admiral Porter ordered Cushing to investigate. On January 18, Cushing went ashore at Fort Caswell, found it abandoned, and raised Old Glory. He soon raised the flag at Smithville as well. He remained there for a week, appointing himself military governor and living in the large, white house he had broken into eight months earlier in the attempt to capture General Hébert.

One of the first things he did in Smithville was to capture the pilots who had guided blockade-runners over the bar. He threatened to hang them unless they hoisted the usual signal lights by which the ships ran in and out. He figured that it would take a few days for news of the fall of Fort Fisher to spread around the world. Meanwhile, an unsuspecting blockade-runner or two might be lured into a trap.

Early in the morning of January 20, lookouts spotted a large steamer signaling to Fort Caswell. For a moment nobody knew what to do, and the steamer appeared ready to depart. Then one of Cushing's officers hailed her. "It's all right," the officer said. "Signal Corps drunk. Great victory. Go ahead."[6] Figuring that the Rebels had beaten off another Yankee attack, the steamer's skipper ordered the vessel to Smithville, where she dropped anchor next to several Union warships. A second steamer soon appeared and was likewise lured toward Smithville. The steamers proved to be the blockade-runners *Stag* and *Charlotte*. Both fell into Union hands.

Cushing led the party that took possession of the *Charlotte*. He recalled:

> When we boarded and informed the captain that his vessel was a prize, he was not the only one astonished. A champagne supper was in progress [in the captain's cabin] in honor of successfully running the blockade at which several English army officers were making merry, confident that they were in the friendly and hospitable bosom of the Southern Confederacy. As we sat down amongst them and ordered the steward to bring another case of champagne, their tongues loosened and one . . . exclaimed, "Beastly luck!"[7]

Like vultures, a number of Union warship skippers claimed credit for capturing the prizes, but Admiral Porter gave the credit to Cushing.

For the next several weeks, Cushing searched for blockade-runners, made small boat raids ashore, and participated in the joint advance up the Cape Fear River on Wilmington. On the night of February 10, Porter ordered him to lead a small boat expedition upriver to gather intelligence on the enemy's defenses. Cushing got within a mile of the city before turning back. He found the river obstructed by a line of heavy piles abreast of Fort Anderson, the last remaining Confederate stronghold on the river, about a third of the way up to Wilmington from Fort Fisher.

The next night Cushing returned to Fort Anderson for a closer look at the obstructions. He found two or three rows of pilings, with sand and earth between them, and numerous torpedoes. He brought the boat to the riverbank, right under the guns of the fort, making a thorough reconnaissance.

Afterward Cushing told Admiral Porter that the obstructions posed a grave hazard to the fleet. Porter knew that many soldiers would die if they had to attack Fort Anderson without naval support. Cushing suggested that they try a ruse, like Porter had done on the Mississippi River. Cushing built a mock monitor out of an old flat boat and some canvas, weighing down one end so that it traveled straight in the five-knot current that ran upriver with the incoming tide.

On February 18, Cushing towed the mock monitor to a position some two hundred yards below the obstructions and cast it loose. The tide carried it right past the fort, reportedly through a hail of Confederate gunfire and a barrage of torpedoes. From the bank the mock monitor looked authentic and formidable. With the Navy flanking them by river and the Army flanking them by land, the Rebels abandoned Fort Anderson that night, not even bothering to spike the ten guns they left behind. Union forces occupied the fort the next morning. Cushing recalled that the Rebel officers he met later "swore like pirates" when they found out that they'd been had.[8]

Cushing hardly had time to stop laughing before Porter ordered him to Norfolk to have a torpedo attached to the *Monticello* in case the Confederate ram *Stonewall,* recently completed at Bordeaux, tried to break the blockade. Cushing left his ship in Norfolk and went on to the Navy Department with dispatches bearing news of the fall of Fort Anderson. While in Washington he visited the White House and regaled the President with the tale of the mock monitor. Lincoln laughed heartily at the story and complimented Cushing for destroying the *Albemarle.* Cushing beamed with pride.

Cushing spent the rest of the war up north. On February 24, Porter signed orders detaching Cushing from the *Monticello,* but Cushing didn't receive them till after the war was over. Meanwhile he went to Boston to visit friends and relatives, then home. News of the fall of Richmond reached Fredonia on April 3. The townspeople mounted a spontaneous celebration at the concert hall, where they sang patriotic songs and made speeches with tears running down their cheeks. A band led part of the group over to the Cushing residence and serenaded the naval hero. Cushing uttered a few choice remarks and called for three cheers. The crowd did so, then escorted Cushing and his mother and sister to the town's leading hostelry for dinner. The Cushings sat at the head of the table, and their fellow townspeople toasted them time and again. Will produced a Confederate flag he had taken from Fort Caswell, and the crowd marched over it in drunken revelry that lasted all night. Lee surrendered a week later, sparking another spontaneous nightlong celebration. Will didn't take part in this one. Instead, he spent the night walking alone over the country roads, thinking of all he had done and all those who were lost.

Cushing found himself adrift in the wake of the war. He was twenty-two years old, had eliminated all doubts about whether he was fit to serve in the Navy, and had emerged alive from the bloodiest war in American history as a national hero. He never doubted that he would remain in the Navy, but he knew that peacetime service would lack the danger, excitement, and freedom from constraint that he had so loved during the war. More ominously, he was suffering from bouts of pain in his hip and back. He began having the attacks a few months after sinking the *Albemarle,* but they were coming more frequently and lasting longer now.

In mid-May he received orders to duty at the Brooklyn navy yard. About a month later, the orders were changed, and he was made executive officer of the *Lancaster,* flagship of the Pacific Squadron. He spent much of the next twenty-one months cruising up and down the West Coast. The highlight of the tour came in March 1866, when the ship stopped at San Francisco and Cushing was given a hero's welcome and "freedom of the city." He reportedly accepted the honor modestly.

Cushing was detached from the *Lancaster* in March 1867 and spent the next eight months awaiting orders. Early spring found him in Fredonia. One windy day in April, he decided to go sailing in Lake Erie with two young female cousins visiting from Boston. Cushing pooh-poohed warnings that the lake was dangerous in such weather and set sail, eager to impress the girls. They had not gone very far before the little boat capsized. A rescue party dodged floating chunks of ice and retrieved the unlucky trio. The girls warmed up beside an open fire and were fine, but Cushing suffered a severe attack of pain in his hip and back, the worst yet.

If Cushing entertained any notion of the incident as sign of his own mortality, he shook it off as the weather warmed. By then a local girl, Katherine Louise Forbes, a close friend of his sister Isabel, had struck his fancy. Kate, in turn, was quite smitten with Will and often sat starry-eyed for hours, while he droned on about his wartime adventures. On July 1, Will asked Kate for her hand in marriage. She said yes.

The couple decided to wait, however, for Will had just gotten new orders. After being shunted about for the rest of the summer, in October he received command of the *Maumee,* slated for a cruise with the Asiatic Squadron. Will was fortunate that Kate was patient, for he was gone two years.

On October 31, 1867, the *Maumee* set sail from the Washington Navy Yard for the Far East, by way of Rio de Janeiro and Cape Town. She arrived at Hong Kong, headquarters of the Asiatic Squadron, on May 1. The squadron commander greeted Cushing warmly and the junior officers were thrilled to have a genuine hero in their midst. The *Maumee* spent the next nineteen months cruising in the China Sea and visiting ports throughout the Far East, including Japan. "Albemarle" Cushing was pleased to learn that his reputation preceded him, even in places like Edo (Tokyo) Bay. In November 1869, both Cushing and his crew were detached from the *Maumee,* and the ship was sold in Hong Kong to save the expense of bringing her home. By this time, the Navy had fallen into one of its periodic "dark ages," with congressional parsimony having reduced it from a wartime high of 671 warships to less than 200, most of them wooden and many of them rotten.

Cushing was glad to leave, for despite frequenting exotic ports of call, his thoughts had early turned to "Kate! Kate!!" as he put it in his private journal of the cruise.[9] He returned to Fredonia that winter, laden with souvenirs and eager to be married. He and Kate tied the knot on February 22, 1870 in what the *Fredonia Censor* described as the most elaborate wedding ceremony ever held in that part of the country in a church brimming with family, friends, and fans.

But not everyone admired Cushing. While Will and Kate were on their honeymoon, the editor of the Jamestown *Journal* attacked him in print, calling him a "little upstart," an "egotistical ass," and "the most ineffable, idiotic young snob that ever trod leather" and declaring that he had "blundered into notoriety."[10] To ensure that Cushing would not miss the editorial, the editor sent copies of the paper to the Navy Department and to prominent Fredonians.

While Cushing received honors modestly, affronts enraged him. Upon returning from his honeymoon, Will and his father-in-law strode into the editor's office. After his father-in-law introduced him, Will lit into the editor with a rawhide whip. It took several office assistants to pull the irate newlywed off of their boss. Afterward, Will and his father-in-law went to dinner at a local hotel, where an officer served them with warrants. The matter was settled out of court.

Cushing returned home and settled comfortably into married life. He showered Kate with gifts, read Thackeray, Dickens, and

Tennyson to her while she did her household chores, and during the social season, accompanied her to their share of balls, parties, and receptions. In the spring of 1870, he was ordered to ordnance duty at the Boston Navy Yard, which he considered "exceedingly dull," as he put it in a letter to a cousin. "We have nothing to do but doze in our office chairs and swear at 'dull Time.'"[11] He rented a little house in Medford and spent many an evening puttering around in the garden. Kate bore him two daughters, Marie Louise and Katherine Abell.

News that Apaches had killed his brother Howard, a lieutenant in the cavalry, on May 5, 1871 darkened Will's tranquil domestic scene. At first, he considered taking leave so he could go to Arizona to fight the Apaches, but a cousin talked him out of it. Stricken with grief, he caught a cold that by the end of the month had developed into pneumonia. Kate nursed him back to health, but it took until the middle of the summer for him to feel better. In November he fell ill again.

News of his promotion to commander on January 31, 1872 brightened his spirits, making him the youngest of that rank in the Navy. The naval hierarchy realized that a morale boost alone couldn't compensate for the ill effects on his health of the Boston climate, so in February he was detached from the navy yard to await orders. He spent the rest of the winter in Washington, D.C., and Norfolk, returning to Fredonia in the spring. The pain in his hip and back had worsened in recent months, and the doctors couldn't help him. He was diagnosed with "sciatica," but the cause of his misery could have been one or more ruptured disks in his spine, tuberculosis of the hip bone, or cancer of the prostate. Whatever it was, he had another breakdown that fall and spent the winter in Fredonia.

Orders in the summer of 1873 to command the *Wyoming* brightened Cushing's spirits, but did not relieve his pain. In August the ship set sail for Aspinwall, on the Isthmus of Panama, by way of Bermuda and Kingston, Jamaica. Civil war had broken out in Panama, and American officials didn't want the isthmian railroad damaged in the fighting. Through constant drilling,

Cushing honed his crew to a fine fighting edge, but the situation never demanded a test of their mettle.

The Caribbean climate improved Cushing's health, and the political situation gave him one last opportunity for action. Revolution had been raging in Cuba for the past five years, the rebels bent on ousting the authority of Spain. In 1870 the insurgents had purchased an American steamer, the *Virginius*, which they used for transporting troops and running guns under the American flag. In October 1873, a Spanish warship intercepted the *Virginius* and brought her to Santiago, where the next month Spanish authorities executed fifty-three of her crew and passengers by firing squad, including many Englishmen and eight Americans.

When news of these events reached the *Wyoming*, Cushing sailed to Kingston to examine the records on file concerning the *Virginius*. At worst, he concluded, the ship was a neutral vessel carrying contraband of war, not a pirate. Cushing soon dropped anchor in the harbor of Santiago, where he dashed off a letter to the Spanish authorities, declaring the execution of Americans taken from the *Virginius* to be "murder" and demanding that the killing stop. He also demanded a meeting with the Spanish general Burriel. When met with an evasive reply, he cleared the *Wyoming* for action and trained her guns on the nearest Spanish warships. "If I do not see General Burriel by the day after tomorrow, and if any more prisoners are executed," he declared, "I shall open fire on the Governor's palace."[12]

"Albemarle" Cushing was not unknown in Spain; General Burriel granted his request. When they met, Cushing refused to shake the general's outstretched hand. "Have I your assurance that no more prisoners will be executed?" asked Cushing.

The general remained silent.

"In that case, sir," said Cushing, "I must request that all the women and children be removed from the city. I would not harm them."

Burriel coughed. He promised to stop the killing, but refused to release the prisoners without orders from Havana. Cushing visited the spot where the executions had taken place, then made plans to free the remaining prisoners by force. Meanwhile, higher authorities on both sides knew that Cushing wouldn't hesitate to start a war, so they quickly hammered out an agreement. A congressional committee later investigated the incident and congratulated Cushing for "upholding the honor of the American flag."[13]

In April 1874, the *Wyoming* returned to Norfolk for extensive repairs, and Cushing was put on a waiting list for reassignment. Cushing went home early the next month. Kate must have been shocked at his appearance. He had fallen ill again over the winter. His eyes were sunk deep into his head, and his body had become painfully thin. Kate thought he looked more like a man of sixty than a man of thirty-one. The pain in his back had become constant, and it made him irritable and short tempered.

The Navy Department gave him an easy assignment, making him executive officer of the Washington Navy Yard. He spent the summer in Washington, D.C., where his wife and daughters afforded him his brightest moments. In August he was appointed senior aide of the navy yard.

On Thanksgiving Day, Will, Kate, and Will's mother, who had arrived earlier that fall for an extended visit, went to church in the morning, spent the afternoon at the Corcoran Gallery of Art, and drove home through a cold rain early that evening for dinner. Cushing didn't enjoy the meal, however, for the pain in his back was worse than ever.

Over Kate's protests, he went to work the following Monday. That evening he staggered home in agony. Morphine injections dulled, but didn't kill, the pain, which drove him into delirium. By December 8, it had become impossible for Kate to take care of her husband and her two little daughters, so Will was moved to the Government Hospital for the Insane. Kate and his mother visited him often, but he often didn't recognize them. On the afternoon of December 17, he regained consciousness and, with outstretched arms, called for his "beloved Kate."[14] With his mother kneeling beside the bed, he and Kate began reciting the

Lord's Prayer together. In the middle of the prayer his voice wavered, and he closed his eyes and died.

The remains were stored temporarily in a vault in the Congressional Cemetery. Across the country, newspapers recounted his deeds. On January 8, 1875, Cushing was buried at the Naval Academy Cemetery, his grave marked by a marble monument bearing the inscription "Albemarle" along one side.

In 1910, Kate Cushing reflected on her husband in a letter to Charles W. Stewart, who was then writing his biography of Will.

> Mr. Cushing was about 6 ft. in height, slender & very erect. He carried his head high and shoulders thrown well back, which gave him a decidedly military air, yet his movements were easy and graceful, and his manner indicated force, strength, & ability. His features were regular and finely cut, his eyes were light blue gray, but his invariable animation & enthusiasm in conversation rendered them dark in appearance. . . . He was of a most affectionate, tender & sympathetic nature. A model husband & father . . . He was deeply religious in his nature and a firm believer in prayer. . . . Mr. Cushing's brilliant mind rendered him a delightful conversationalist. He was a fluent and charming writer. All his impulses were fine, noble. He was generous to a fault.

She added a year later in another letter, "He had a magnetic personality that one felt as soon as he approached."[15]

Adm. David Dixon Porter wrote in his often inaccurate naval history of the Civil War that Cushing "made a name for himself by his total disregard of danger" and by his "fancy for seeking adventures." Porter couldn't help but admire him, even if grudgingly and with faint praise. Cushing was "brave to recklessness," said the admiral.

> [He] seemed more like a free-lance than a regular officer of the Navy, educated in the school of routine, and, in fact, the restraints of discipline were irksome to him. . . . [He] was always ready to perform any act of daring; and although he was not always successful, the honor of the flag never suffered at his hands. There were plenty of young officers in the Navy who were equally brave, and with

more judgement, but Cushing was of a peculiar temperament, always doing something to astonish his commanders, and whether fortunate or not in his undertakings, he was sure to create a sensation. . . . Cushing's hazardous undertakings were sometimes criticized as useless, but there was more method in them than appeared on the surface, and important information was sometimes obtained, to say nothing of the brilliant example of courage and enterprise which they afforded to others.[16]

William Barker Cushing executed the Civil War's most daring small-unit naval operations behind enemy lines. Like the special operations conducted by today's Navy SEALs, Cushing's shallow-water and riverine boat operations, counterguerrilla operations, punitive expeditions, and intelligence-gathering missions depended on stealth, surprise, and speed for success.

They also depended on audacity. Indeed, audacity was Cushing's most prominent attribute, followed by utter fearlessness. He also had a large ego, born of his tremendous abilities and constant need to prove himself. He behaved modestly in the face of compliments, but insults outraged him. He believed in authority, but felt that those who had it had to earn it. Nothing aroused his disdain more than a superior officer who was afraid to act or whose character he felt lacked some essential ingredient.

During the war, Cushing was always concocting schemes that his superiors denounced as foolish. Porter was right to say that there was a certain amount of recklessness in him. At best, his blatant disregard for the safety of his men can be explained by the hubris and feeling of invincibility that resulted from his youth and amazing success.

Yet, even Porter admitted that there was method to his madness. As Gideon Welles put it, Cushing's exploits embodied "not only audacity and intrepid courage, but wonderful sagacity and prudence. Projects which most persons deemed wild and inconsiderate will be found on investigation to have been deliberate and well planned designs."[17] Whether a given mission was well thought out, as in the case of the *Albemarle* raid, or improvised, as in the case of the Chuckatuck raid, Cushing always came out alive because he could think on his feet, retain the initiative, and keep the enemy off balance. And he was blessed with an almost unbelievable amount of luck.

You'd think that sailors would have dropped like flies around him but, miraculously, most of the men under his command during missions behind enemy lines managed to come out alive, too, even during the *Albemarle* raid. Cushing "never failed to procure an abundance of volunteers for his most hazardous expeditions," declared Gideon Welles, "notwithstanding his juvenile looks and manner." As Welles put it, Cushing possessed "the happy faculty of magnetizing and inspiring others."[18]

John W. Grattan, who served on Porter's staff and got to know Cushing personally, echoed this view in his memoirs.

> Cushing was a strict disciplinarian, but in spite of his strong will and apparent harshness the sailors fairly worshipped him. His smooth beardless face always wore a smile except when annoyed or engaged on dangerous service, when it would change into a settled frown. His blue eyes always had a determined and fearless look and his coolness and self possession was the subject of many remarks. When not on duty and in the privacy of our wardroom he was as jolly and free as a schoolboy; could sing a few sailor songs and ballads and tell a good yarn or laugh heartily at a good joke. One of his principal characteristics was his extreme modesty in the presence of strangers and he very rarely spoke of his daring achievements and never in a spirit of braggadocio.[19]

Not everyone shared these feelings. "Cushing was a very peculiar man," recalled John C. Howard, who served with him on the *Albemarle* raid. "He had no close friends or intimates. He was always by himself. To those he liked he would be civil, but he would go to any extent to injure his enemies, of whom he had plenty."[20]

Cushing's preferred solution to most problems involved action and violence. He especially loved the "wild pleasure and excitement" he felt while in combat. He loved war and being at sea, but seemed adrift on shore and in time of peace.

Notes

CCCHS   William B. Cushing papers, Chautauqua County Historical Society, Westfield, New York.

CSHSW   William B. Cushing letters, State Historical Society of
Wisconsin, Madison, Wisconsin.

ORN   U.S. Department of the Navy, *Official Records of the
Union and Confederate Navies in the War of the Rebellion*, 31
vols. Washington, D.C.: Government Printing Office,
1894–1922. All citations are to Series 1.

ZBC   ZB files, s.v. "Cushing, William B.," Navy Department
Library, Washington, D.C.

Preface

1. "Francis H. Swan's Account of William B. Cushing's Torpedoing
   of Albemarle Oct. 1864," box 24, Dudley Wright Knox papers,
   Library of Congress.
2. William B. Cushing, "Outline Story of the War Experiences of
   William B. Cushing As Told by Himself," *United States Naval
   Institute Proceedings* 38 (September 1912), 946.
3. Ralph J. Roske and Charles Van Doren, *Lincoln's Commando:
   The Biography of Cdr. William B. Cushing, USN* (Annapolis:
   Naval Institute Press, 1995), 280.
4. "Francis H. Swan's Account," Library of Congress.

Chapter 1

1. Eliza Mary Hatch Edwards, *Commander William Barker Cushing
   of the United States Navy* (New York: F. Tennyson Neely, 1898),
   9.

2. Ibid., 13.
3. Ibid., 29–30.
4. Ibid., 35.
5. Roske and Van Doren, *Lincoln's Commando,* 58.
6. Ibid.

Chapter 2
1. The statistical data on Cushing's contemporaries at the Naval Academy comes from the United States Naval Academy Alumni Association, Inc., *Register of Alumni: Graduates and Former Naval Cadets and Midshipmen,* vol. 1 (Annapolis: Naval Academy Alumni Association Inc., 1995), 33–37.
2. George Dewey, *Autobiography of George Dewey: Admiral of the Navy* (New York: Scribner, 1913), 16–17.
3. Thomas O. Selfridge Jr., *Memoirs of Thomas O. Selfridge, Jr., Rear Admiral U.S.N.* (New York: G. P. Putnam's Sons, 1924), 287.
4. William Cushing to Mary Edwards, May 20, 1860, CSHSW.
5. Ibid., November 25, 1860.
6. Ibid., October 15, 1860.
7. Roske and Van Doren, *Lincoln's Commando,* 65.
8. Charles Todorich, *The Spirited Years: A History of the Antebellum Naval Academy* (Annapolis: Naval Institute Press, 1984), 139.
9. Roske and Van Doren, *Lincoln's Commando,* 67.
10. Ibid., 63.
11. William Cushing to Mary Edwards, May 20, 1860.
12. Ibid., October 15, 1860.
13. Robley D. Evans, *A Sailor's Log: Recollections of Forty Years of Naval Life* (New York: D. Appleton and Co., 1901), 39.
14. Todorich, *The Spirited Years,* 190.
15. William Cushing to Mary Edwards, December 12, 1860.
16. Ibid., January 18, 1859.
17. Roske and Van Doren, *Lincoln's Commando,* 73.
18. William Cushing to Mary Edwards, December 12, 1860.
19. Ibid., December 17, 1860.
20. Ibid.
21. Ibid., December 12, 1860.
22. Ibid., May 20, 1860; William Cushing to Mary Cushing, May 14, 1864, CCCHS.

23. Cushing, "War Experiences," 941.
24. William Cushing to Mary Edwards, December 22, 1860, CSHSW.
25. Charles W. Stewart, "William Barker Cushing," *United States Naval Institute Proceedings* 38 (September 1912), 428; Roske and Van Doren, *Lincoln's Commando*, 88.
26. Stewart, "Cushing," 428.
27. Welles to Dorr, February 17, 1876, ZBC.
28. Stewart, "Cushing," 429.
29. Cushing, "War Experiences," 947.
30. Welles to Dorr, February 17, 1876, ZBC.
31. Ibid.

Chapter 3

1. Roske and Van Doren, *Lincoln's Commando,* 95.
2. William Cushing to Mary Edwards, May 7, 1861.
3. William Cushing to Mary Cushing, May 24, 1861, in Stewart, "Cushing," 431–32.
4. William Cushing to Mary Edwards, June 25, 1861, CSHSW.
5. ORN 6: 35.
6. William Cushing to Mary Edwards, July 31, 1861, CSHSW.
7. Ibid.
8. Ibid., August 17, 1861.
9. Stewart, "Cushing," 431.
10. Cushing, "War Experiences," 942.
11. Ibid., 943.
12. ORN, 6: 127.
13. Stewart, "Cushing," 431.
14. Stringham to Fox, September 11, 1861, ZBC.
15. Cushing to Stringham, September 29, 1861, and Stringham to Cushing, October 8, 1861, ZBC.
16. Welles to Dorr, February 17, 1876, ZBC.
17. Blake to Welles, October 15, 1861, ZBC.
18. William Cushing to Mary Edwards, November 22, 1861, CSHSW.
19. Cushing, "War Experiences," 945; William Cushing to Mary Edwards, November 22, 1861.
20. Cushing, "War Experiences," 945.
21. Robert J. Schneller Jr., *A Quest for Glory: A Biography of Rear*

Admiral John A. Dahlgren (Annapolis: Naval Institute Press, 1996), 197.

22. Cushing, "War Experiences," 945–46.

23. Ibid., 946.

24. Fox to Goldsborough, March 27, 1862; Robert Means Thompson and Richard Wainwright, eds., *Confidential Correspondence of Gustavus Vasa Fox*, vol. 2 (New York: De Vinne Press, 1918), 255.

25. Cushing, "War Experiences," 946.

26. William Cushing to Mary Cushing, August 30, 1862, CCCHS.

27. William Cushing to Mary Cushing, August 20, 1862, quoted in Stewart, "Cushing," 433; William Cushing to Mary Cushing, August 30, 1862.

28. ORN 8: 104, 109.

29. William Cushing to Mary Edwards, October 18, 1862, CSHSW.

30. Ibid.

31. ORN 8: 151–152; William Cushing to Mary Edwards, October 18, 1862.

32. ORN 8: 174.

33. Ibid., 232.

34. Ibid.

35. ORN 8: 231–32.

36. Cushing, "War Experiences," 952.

37. Thompson and Wainwright, *Confidential Correspondence*, 238.

38. Ibid., 236.

39. ORN 8: 403.

40. Cushing, "War Experiences," 953.

41. ORN 8: 403.

42. William Cushing to Mary Edwards, April 5, 1863, CSHSW.

43. Ibid.

44. Ibid.

45. Cushing to Davenport, April 3, 1863, ZBC.

46. ORN 8: 729.

47. Ibid., 713.

48. Ibid., 723–24.

49. Ibid.

50. Ibid., 734.

51. Cushing, "War Experiences," 958.

52. ORN 8: 772, 774–75.

53. Ibid., 789.
54. William Cushing to Mary Edwards, June 21, 1863, CSHSW.
55. Ibid.
56. Ibid.

Chapter 4

1. Emory M. Thomas, *Robert E. Lee: A Biography* (New York: W. W. Norton, 1995), 288.
2. Roske and Van Doren, *Lincoln's Commando,* 173.
3. Cushing, "War Experiences," 963.
4. William Cushing to Mary Cushing, July 30, 1863, CCCHS.
5. Cushing, "War Experiences," 964.
6. Ibid., 965.
7. ORN 9: 184.
8. Cushing, "War Experiences," 965.
9. Ibid., 965–66.
10. Ibid., 967.
11. Ibid.
12. Ibid., 969.
13. Welles to Cushing, March 31, 1864, CCCHS.
14. Thompson and Wainwright, *Confidential Correspondence,* 279–80.
15. Ibid.; Stewart, "Cushing," 463.
16. ORN 10: 39–40.
17. Ibid., 128.
18. Cushing, "War Experiences," 970.
19. Ibid., 971.
20. Ibid., 971–72.
21. Glenn Howell, "Picnic with Cushing," *United States Naval Institute Proceedings* 62 (August 1936), 1101.
22. ORN 10: 417–18.
23. Ibid., 451–53.
24. Ibid., 460–61.
25. Ibid., 247.
26. Cushing, "War Experiences," 974–75.
27. Ibid., 975.
28. Ibid.
29. *The Fredonia Censor,* May 28, 1897, CCCHS.
30. Cushing, "War Experiences," 975.

31. David D. Porter, *The Naval History of the Civil War* (1886; reprint, Secaucus, N.J.: Castle, 1984), 472.
32. Welles to Cushing, October 19, 1864, ZBC.
33. ORN 10: 594.
34. Accounts differ as to the exact date. This account is based on ORN 10: 569.
35. "Francis H. Swan's Account" box 24.
36. Cushing, "War Experiences," 977.
37. ORN 10: 613.
38. Ibid.
39. Cushing, "War Experiences," 981.
40. ORN 10: 618.
41. *The Fredonia Censor*, May 26, 1897.

Chapter 5

1. Stewart, "Cushing," 490.
2. Ibid., 490.
3. ORN 11: 258.
4. Roske and Van Doren, *Lincoln's Commando*, 260.
5. Cushing, "War Experiences," 987.
6. John W. Grattan, *Under the Blue Pennant or Notes of a Naval Officer, 1863–1865*, ed. Robert J. Schneller Jr. (New York: Wiley, 1999), 180.
7. Cushing, "War Experiences," 988.
8. Ibid., 991.
9. Cushing, "Private Journal," May 6, 1868, CCCHS.
10. Roske and Van Doren, *Lincoln's Commando*, 280.
11. Cushing to John Elliot Pillsbury, April 18, 1871, ZBC.
12. Roske and Van Doren, *Lincoln's Commando*, 291.
13. Ibid., 294.
14. Katherine Louise Forbes Cushing, "Copies of Letters," CCCHS.
15. Ibid.
16. Porter, *Naval History*, 401, 403, 472, 473, 478.
17. Welles to Dorr, February 17, 1876, ZBC.
18. Ibid.
19. Grattan, *Under the Blue Pennant*, 143–44.
20. Unprovenanced newspaper clipping entitled "Fought with Cushing," CSHSW.

Bibliographic Note

The purpose of this bibliography is to tell readers who want to know more about Cushing where to look. No attempt has been made to reproduce the title of every work cited in the endnotes or used in writing the book.

The forthcoming biography of Cushing by Chris Fonvielle promises to be the best work yet written on the man. The best biography of Cushing now in print is Ralph J. Roske and Charles Van Doren's *Lincoln's Commando: The Biography of Cdr. William B. Cushing* (Annapolis: Naval Institute Press, 1995). Their book is a model of historical storytelling and reads more like a novel than a scholarly biography. Its principal flaw is its lack of footnotes and bibliography.

Roske and Van Doren drew much of their material from two more nearly contemporary book-length biographies: Eliza Mary Hatch Edwards's *Commander William Barker Cushing of the United States Navy* (New York: F. Tennyson Neely, 1898) and Theron Wilber Haight's *Three Wisconsin Cushings* (Madison: Wisconsin Historical Commission, 1910). Edwards knew Cushing and his mother, siblings, wife, and daughters personally. Cushing's letters and the recollections of those who knew him constitute much of her book. Haight based much of his work on hers.

Early in the last century the *United States Naval Institute Proceedings* published in two installments (vol. 38, June and September 1912) a short biographical sketch of Cushing by Charles W. Stewart, superintendent of the Office of Library and Naval War Records, forerunner to today's Navy Department Library. The piece includes numerous extracts from the official records and is based in part on the author's correspondence with Cushing's family and contemporaries, but it leans more toward hagiography than biography. The September 1912 issue of the *Proceedings* also includes the "Outline Story of the War Experiences of William B. Cushing As Told By Himself," which Cushing wrote in 1869–70. Cushing based the memoir on a journal he kept during the war, which is available in Record Group 45 of the National Archives in Washington, D.C.

Most of Cushing's official wartime correspondence appears in *Official Records of the Union and Confederate Navies in the War of the Rebellion*, eds. Richard Rush et al., 31 vols. (Washington: Government Printing Office, 1894–1922). Cushing's account of the *Albemarle* raid is presented in *Battles and Leaders of the Civil War*, eds. Robert Underwood Johnson and Clarence Clough Buel, 4 vols. (New York: Century, 1887).

The principal collections of Cushing manuscripts reside in the Chautauqua County Historical Society in Westfield, New York; the State Historical Society of Wisconsin in Madison, Wisconsin; and the Navy Department Library in Washington, D.C. Other Cushing papers are scattered across the United States in public repositories and private collections too numerous to list here.

The most comprehensive reference work on "Uncle Sam's Web-feet," as Lincoln put it, is the *Civil War Naval Chronology, 1861–1865* (Washington, D.C.: Government Printing Office, 1971), published by the Navy Department's Naval History Division, now the Naval Historical Center. Few chronologies reach the level of detail provided in its daily entries, and it is chock full of illustrations, appendices, and trivia to boot.

Two of the best bibliographic works on all aspects of the Civil War are *Writing the Civil War: The Quest to Understand*, eds.

James M. McPherson and William J. Cooper Jr. (Columbia: University of South Carolina Press, 1998), and David J. Eicher's *The Civil War in Books: An Analytical Bibliography* (Chicago: University of Illinois Press, 1997). Either one will take you wherever you want to go in the Civil War.

Index

About the Author

Robert J. Schneller Jr., Ph.D., is a historian in the Contemporary History Branch of the U.S. Naval Historical Center. Schneller's first book, *A Quest for Glory: A Biography of Rear Admiral John A. Dahlgren*, received the 1996 John Lyman Book Award in Biography from the North American Society for Oceanic History. He also is the coauthor (with Edward J. Marolda) of *Shield and Sword: The United States Navy and the Persian Gulf War*, which received the prestigious Theodore and Franklin D. Roosevelt Naval History Prize from the Navy League of the United States. Schneller's other books include an edition of John W. Grattan's Civil War memoir, *Under the Blue Pennant, or Notes of a Naval Officer, 1863–1865* and *Farragut: America's First Admiral*, the initial volume in Brassey's Military Profiles series. He lives in Lake Ridge, Virginia.

MILITARY PROFILES
AVAILABLE

Farragut: America's First Admiral
Robert J. Schneller Jr.

Drake: For God, Queen, and Plunder
Wade G. Dudley

Santa Anna: A Curse upon Mexico
Robert L. Scheina

Eisenhower: Soldier-Statesman of the American Century
Douglas Kinnard

Semmes: Rebel Raider
John M. Taylor

Doolittle: Aerospace Visionary
Dik Alan Daso

Foch: Supreme Allied Commander in the Great War
Michael S. Neiberg

Villa: Soldier of the Mexican Revolution
Robert L. Scheina

Cushing: Civil War SEAL
Robert J. Schneller Jr.

Alexander the Great: Invincible King of Macedonia
Peter G. Tsouras

MILITARY PROFILES
FORTHCOMING
Meade
Richard A. Sauers
Halsey
Robert J. Cressman
Rickover
Norman Polmar and Thomas B. Allen
Tirpitz
Michael Epkenhans